Piercing the Mist

PIERCING THE MIST

Glimpses of God in the Wonders of Life

Leo Holland

LIGUORI
PUBLICATIONS

One Liguori Drive
Liguori, MO 63057-9999
(314) 464-2500

ISBN 0-89243-526-7
Library of Congress Catalog Card Number: 93-77523

Copyright © 1993, Liguori Publications
Printed in the United States of America

Scripture quotations are taken from THE NEW AMERICAN BIBLE WITH REVISED NEW TESTAMENT, copyright © 1989, AND THE REVISED PSALMS, copyright © 1991, by the Confraternity of Christian Doctrine, Washington, D.C., and are used with permission. All rights reserved.

Cover and interior art by Christine Kraus

For
My Father

CONTENTS

ACKNOWLEDGMENTS

The reflections in this book were not planned, programmed, and mosaically set in place. They came like water springing from a rock—surprising but wonderful.

I am grateful to the Holy Spirit for sending these little stories and minidramas, for flashing images in my mind, and for writing prayerful words on my heart.

Special thanks and love go to my spiritual benefactors—those men and women, boys and girls, who shaped and formed my conscience, imagination, and vision.

They loved me in teaching and evangelizing ways. I hope much of their spirit emerges in these pages, that it touches and renews your heart as it did mine.

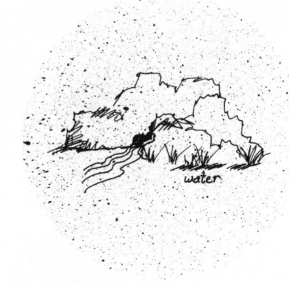

water

INTRODUCTION

I walked slowly up the small rise. I was alone on a pleasant stroll to nowhere. It was sunny, cloudless, and almost cool. A faint breeze ran across my cheek.

As I topped the rise, a majestic sheet of wildflowers popped up magically below me. They covered an acre.

The blending of colors, the harmony of varieties, and the continuous waves of rhythm on the nodding surface fused into a loveliness that was stunning.

The tableau was outrageously and exquisitely beautiful. The blooms were deeply and delicately organic in mood and impression, but in spite of my joy, I felt a frustration at not being able to grasp it fully, to absorb and incarnate it—that something more.

It was, quite simply, beyond me. I was overcome by wonder, feebly reaching out for something outside my powers and capabilities. But it was a sweet frustration, a comfortable awe. To perceive even the hem of the garment, to grasp some small measure of the splendor, was a precious gift. I stood there for a long time—full of looking.

God conveys loveliness, sweetness, and goodness—always and everywhere—to every heart and mind. It is a continual cherishing. Every spiritually alert and open heart experiences love—touches from the Lord, vivid perceptions of God in our world.

The spiritually blind see the concrete and the immediate—only the surface. With grace, we possess second sight—the ability to see beneath the veil of phenomena into the heart and soul of reality.

God calls us to observe his repeated emergence in our surroundings, to discover him in the unnoticed glories of the day-to-day. He calls us to pierce the mist of the mundane, to rejoice with him in the hidden splendor of his creation, in the inner beauty of all creatures and created things.

PIERCING THE MIST

Whoever believes in the Son of God has this testimony within himself.

1 John 5:10

We camped for a week on an island off the coast of Maine. It was a family vacation in a magical place. The island was summer—lush and incredibly green. Beautiful ferns—two to three feet high—grew everywhere.

Sometimes the fog would come in. We could see it from a long way off—rolling forward, probing the forest, enveloping us finally in a faintly damp, diaphanous veil.

I awoke early one morning and slipped quietly out of our tent into the foggy forest. There was a strangeness in the morning silence. I felt a momentary sense of deep aloneness, a tense eeriness. Suddenly, I was startled by a rustling in the brush, almost under my feet, and I heard faint, steady sounds in the distance. After a long moment my son Jim came jogging down the path to our campsite, appearing magically and wonderfully out of the mist.

A widely pervasive moral mist inhabits our lives. There is an uncomfortable mix of good and evil in our hearts and in the hearts and minds of those around us.

Goodness is familiar. Sometimes it emerges powerfully in our lives, like Jim emerged from the mist that day. When that happens, our deep needs of the moment are met with kindness, compassion, and unselfish love. On occasion we are called to minister love and patient help to others. God presents us to one another, in love, as a gift of glory.

Evil is equally familiar. We are threatened, intimidated, and besieged by temptations and our own weaknesses. There is a tense eeriness about these moments of spiritual danger that can be dispelled by prayer and surrendering the moment to God.

When we prayerfully surrender our hearts to God, Jesus responds. He appears magically and wonderfully out of the moral mist. His light pierces the darkness of our fears and uncertainties. His love lightens and illuminates our hearts. His strength becomes ours.

Jesus, you are the light that dims the sun. You are the love that surpasses saints and angels. You are the glory of the Father. Pierce the mist that surrounds me, Lord. Fill me with yourself. Live in my heart.

fern

ROSE BLANKET

God is light, and in him there is no
darkness at all.

1 John 1:5

At midday in midsummer, the Florida sun can be hot and merciless. You can see its power in the blinding glare from the white sand. Heat waves are visible to the naked eye. They rise in wavy patterns from the roads like steam from a boiling kettle.

At sunset something happens; a magic change occurs. The light softens and diffuses. Everything seems covered with a rose blanket—a shade lighter here, a hue darker there, but of one weave, one substance. People sometimes stop. They stand and marvel at the splendor.

God's grace, his help, the aid he sends, the light that lights our way, is neither blindingly harsh nor shadowy and indistinct. It is, rather, pervasive and penetrating. It reaches out everywhere and to everyone. It enters the surface and texture of our lives. It takes up residence in our souls. It grows there.

Sometimes we feel a harsh heat in God's grace. It seems to burn our minds and souls. What we are experiencing is conviction—a realization of our sinfulness. At other times, God's light seems shadowed and diffi-

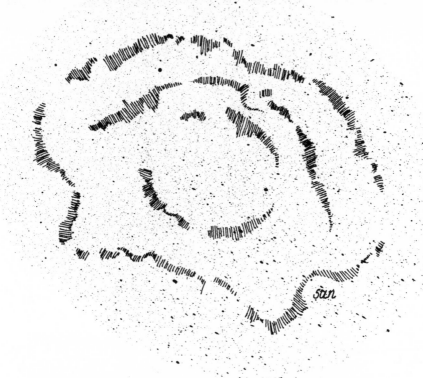

san

cult to grasp. What we are experiencing at those times are the barriers of our egotism and our intense human striving, the draining distraction of the day-to-day.

God sees the inner heart. He knows us well, our strengths and our weaknesses. Most of all, he knows our needs. And he sends his rose blanket of love and grace to each of us daily as a healing remedy, a source of spiritual power, and an eternal and timeless blessing.

Holy Spirit, you know how confused I can be, how tentative, how unsure. Give me the grace to see the unspeakable beauty and power of your gifts. Help me to remain open and eager to receive and submit to your truth and to witness to others of God's searching love and patient mercy toward them.

THE DEER AT EMERALD BAY

I have decided to lead you
up out of the misery of Egypt [into]...
a land flowing with milk and honey.

Exodus 3:17

Waterton, in the Canadian Rockies, is a small town on the shores of Emerald Bay. On a sunny Saturday morning I hunted for souvenirs in the several blocks of shops at the center of town.

As I emerged from a small gift shop, my attention was taken by an unfamiliar clopping sound. I turned and was surprised to see fifteen or twenty deer trotting down the main street.

Cars stopped. Conversations ceased. The deer moved into the center of an intersection and milled about nervously. Their high-strung intensity was unsettling. They were confused and out of place.

Everyone waited patiently, silently praying that none of the animals would bolt. In a primitive panic, they could run headlong into a plate-glass window or smash their bodies against an unfamiliar obstacle. After a long moment, what was obviously the lead animal began to trot slowly back up the street toward the wooded mountain area. The rest of the group followed, heading toward safe and familiar ground.

All of us sometimes find ourselves in morally threatening situations. In these environments, we frequently feel confused and uncertain. Negative peer pressure can be powerful. Evil can be presented attractively. We realize that we are out of place. We are spiritually besieged.

God sees our dilemmas, and his heart is open to us. He is, in fact, always present and always active. He led the Jewish people out of the wilderness, and he will lead us out of every difficulty if we call on him with a sincere and trusting heart. His strength is ours, his peace is ours, and—most importantly—we are his. We are sons and daughters whom God calls and leads to safe, holy, and familiar ground.

Father, your inspiration, guidance, and direction give us vision and light, a way out of every difficulty. I thank you for the merciful grace of knowing and asking and for the unutterable joy of receiving.

DANCING LEAVES

Now the Lord is the Spirit, and where the
Spirit of the Lord is, there is freedom.

2 Corinthians 3:17

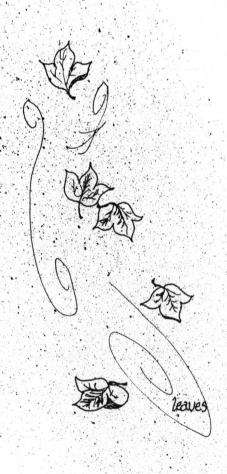

leaves

Through the sliding-glass doors I could see thousands of leaves swirling, leaping, and pirouetting. Driven by the gusty fall winds, they were like mad dancers in a frenzied ballet.

In spite of an undeniable impression of virtuosity—of each leaf attempting to outdo the others in its sudden, erratic movements—there was little real individuality in the whirling mass of autumn leaves. Their movements depended totally on an external motive force. When the wind stopped, they stopped.

God has given us the gift of freedom, of choice, of self-determination. We, on the other hand, can choose to dance the spiritual dance of life or death. We can generate goodness or evil in ourselves and strongly influence the lives of others. We can create a heaven or a hell here and now. We have a dignity that can be our destruction.

God respects our freedom, but he calls us into his arms. He seeks our loving surrender to the dance that blesses, that affirms, and that endures.

Lord God, that you share your divine life and power with us is awesome and intimidating. Some men and women close their eyes to the dignity and glory that their daily lives and simple acts can generate. Open their minds and hearts, Lord. Help them to understand their creative power of love. Help them to rejoice in choosing a love that is active and loyal.

FULL BLESSING

*Lift up your heads, O gates;
rise up, you ancient portals,
that the king of glory may enter.*

Psalm 24:7

Claire sat in the waiting room on an uncomfortable aluminum chair with black plastic cushions. The antiseptic odors of the hospital felt vaguely threatening. Her only companion, an older man in a faded blue jacket, was sound asleep, snoring faintly. *It's so hot in here*, Claire thought. *How can he sleep with that jacket on?*

She turned away from her companion to better concentrate on her pain and fear, the growing sense of doom and loss that was in her. Just down the hall, a few feet away, her mother was dying.

Claire and her mother had always been close. In many ways, they were like sisters, sharing the same convictions and biases, the same sense of humor, the same point of view. All of that had changed, however, in the last hour. Now her mother was old and sick, someone from a different generation, someone who was slipping slowly away.

Claire felt betrayed, outraged, and angered. She sobbed quietly, the emptiness within her enormous and dark. Her breathing became tight and shallow as her pain burst out violently. She shouted, "God help

holy spirit

me!" For a moment, she felt naked and foolish. She looked around to see if anyone had heard her. The man in the blue jacket slept peacefully. No one else was there.

Suddenly, she felt an inner fire, a warm glow that moved slowly through her body, bringing with it a deep peace. Claire felt joyful and relaxed. Yet with this strange euphoria came a momentary sense of guilt. Then it struck her like a thunderbolt: this glow—this heat—was simply God in her. His love, the power of the Holy Spirit, was comforting her—giving her power to bear the unbearable. She surrendered to God's peace.

Later Claire told me, "I think that God is always there in the fullness of his power, but we are not always fully present to him. A deep need or pain, even a disaster, can sometimes open our hearts to his full blessing. That's what happened to me the night my mother died."

Give me the grace, Father, to remember you, to consecrate a special time of prayer to you each day. I want to open my heart and surrender my mind to your majesty, power, and love. I want the fullness of your blessing to descend upon me and enter into my spirit. For your Father's heart and merciful love, I praise and thank you.

TURNABOUT

The LORD is trustworthy in every word...
and raises up all who are bowed down.
You, LORD, watch over
all who love you....

Psalm 145:13-14, 20

While meditating, I had fallen into a reverie. I seemed to be walking at evening through the narrow streets of a small medieval town. Stone buildings cast heavy shadows in the narrow winding streets. The only light came from an occasional lantern.

As I made one of the many winding turns, I glimpsed a large wicker basket in a shadowed doorway. In the dim light that centered on the basket, I saw what appeared to be the baby Jesus, abandoned and alone. Rushing forward with concern and compassion, I bent over the basket and saw with a shock that the baby was not Jesus, after all. It was me!

Suddenly, Jesus did appear, moving forward out of the shadow of the doorway. He was dressed in a rough woolen robe with a hood. Looking at me lovingly, he bent down, picked up the basket, and turned and walked up the stairway into what was clearly his Father's house. I was stunned by the rapid turnabout.

When we rush forward with concern and compassion to minister love and support to the oppressed, abandoned, and needy brothers and sisters of Jesus, he reciprocates in power. He responds to our little love-offerings with a tidal wave of divine love, protection, and healing. He blesses us with the blessing we have given to others.

Jesus, receive my prayers and love, my patience and little
sacrifices, my fidelity and commitment to you. We
desire, Lord, to minister love to you—on the cross at
Gethsemane—to be loyal and faithful so that we may one
day share fully in your glory.

UNFOLDING VISTAS

Like a shepherd he feeds his flock;
in his arms he gathers the lambs....

Isaiah 40:11

As we drove along the Oregon coast, the low rolling mountains and the rugged coastline provided one breathtaking view after another. The curving roads presented a seemingly endless series of unfolding vistas that turned my mind to thoughts of God's goodness and creative generosity.

To savor God's gifts, to experience the full glory of the Oregon coast, you have to know when to stop and let the unique beauty of special scenes soak into your memory bank. Too many of us race through life with scarcely a side-glance at the really important values in our lives. When we do stop, it may be for the wrong reasons or because we are tired or sick or discouraged. Too frequently, we are trying to make our own way, to do it all—all by ourselves—and we become exhausted.

True wisdom means more than taking time to smell the flowers. It is seeing the flowers as a gift that opens the door to wisdom. Prayer time with our generous God can lead us to a deep knowledge and appreciation of the many good gifts that surround us and the spiritual vistas to which God is calling us. We will come to learn that God desires daily intimate time with us, that he wants to counsel, warn, guide, and protect us, to enlighten our hearts and minds.

We don't have to do it all, all by ourselves. God's greatest gift to us is his always active, undergirding grace and power. He wants to share our burdens—to carry us beyond temptations, fears, and doubts to sanity and safety, to strength and victory.

Jesus, give me the grace to live a life close to you, hearing your voice, seeing your beauty in creation, and rejoicing in your friendship, power, and love. Let me always be conscious of your nearness, your help, and your strength that is mine.

Jesus

DIFFERENT GODS

"And I have given them the glory you gave me, so that they may be one, as we are one...."

John 17:22

A character in a play, observing how children seem protected from danger in a special way, commented, "There's a special God for children."

As we look at the broad spectrum of human activity and the even wider span of God's providence, it seems that there are quite a large number of special Gods.

It is not difficult to understand why primitive men and women came to a belief in polytheism. They saw God emerging powerfully and episodically in their lives and assumed that a different spirit was emerging each time.

We know through revelation that there is one God, that our one God consists of three Persons in the mystery of the Holy Trinity, and that our God has a million faces of love.

Anne, a very dear friend, used to pray with great fervor and intensity, "Jesus, you are *my* Lord and *my* God." The beauty, joy, and wonder of our Christian faith is that we can all say that same prayer because there is a special God for you and me—for each of us. His name is Jesus, and his face for you is unconditional love.

Jesus, intimacy is difficult for many men and women, seemingly impossible for some. Yet in our hearts we all yearn to possess and to be possessed in love. Thank you, Lord, for your universal, gentle, sweet, and holy call to love. Release the fullness of your grace, divine Savior. Draw all men and women to your embrace. Fold us all in the unity of your Spirit that we may be one as you are one with the Father.

A DARK AND LONELY ROAD

*Do everything without grumbling or
questioning, that you may be blameless and
innocent, children of God without blemish in
the midst of a crooked and perverse generation,
among whom you shine like lights in the
world....*

Philippians 2:14-15

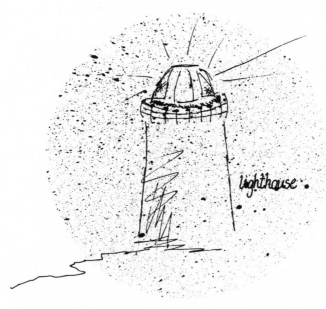

lighthouse .

I was driving along a coastal highway at three
o'clock in the morning, heading back north from our
Florida vacation. It was quiet. Everyone in the family
was asleep. The tires hummed a lonely lullaby on the
damp highway. The headlight beams were like two
knives piercing the darkness.

Up ahead, far off in the distance, a light came on
and went off at five-second intervals. It may have been
a lighthouse or a transmission tower, but I know it was
the result of some human action. It carried a small tinge

of the personal. As little as it was, it was comforting on that dark and lonely road.

God's call differs radically from person to person and from time to time. At one extreme, a small number of men and women are called to major public ministries. At the other end of the spectrum, many of us wonder if we are called at all. No invitation seems to emerge strongly and clearly in our consciousness. We feel vaguely dissatisfied. We are anxious to learn, to serve, and to grow.

God has a plan for every life. For most of us, that plan is simple and humble. It is meant to unfold in our families and neighborhoods. Taking time to listen, an embrace, a smile, a word of compassion and understanding—these are small gifts we can distribute in living out God's plan for our lives.

As much as we would like to, we cannot do great things for our great God. We are grains of sand on the vast earth. We are tiny and weak. But in the daily personal encounters of our lives, we can all be lights of Christ.

We can give comfort on a dark and lonely road. God will see our light in the darkness, and he will bless us. We can touch his heart with gifts that are small, that are tiny but precious.

Jesus, you know how much I seek signs of your approval, marks of your love. Teach me to live by faith, trusting in your promises. Give me the grace to believe everything, to hope everything, and joyfully to accept anything—from your divine heart of love and mercy.

SNOWY MORNING

For he says to the snow, "Fall to the earth...."

Job 37:6

It had been snowing all morning, the kind of wet, heavy snow that bends branches and slides thickly underfoot.

I watched the gilding of our garden from the warm vantage point of our den. The snow was accumulating on the trees. Periodically, a clump of snow would begin to slide from a branch, then fall to earth. All over the yard, little clumps of snow were falling.

I was impressed not so much by the falling snow as by the pervasive force of gravity. The ground seemed to *attract* the snow as if it had some special need for it.

God's goodness is rich and productive. It overflows; we see it in his creation. We also see it when we pray, when we seek his help. Through God's tender mercy, his grace falls on us—like clumps of snow—with redeeming love and transforming power.

We are like the earth that attracts and receives the snow. We have a craving in our hearts, an emptiness that attracts God's love. He loves us so greatly because we need him so much.

Lord God, you have made us for yourself.
True victory for each of us lies in you
and your plan for our lives. We
rejoice, Lord, in our destiny, in
our lurching and awkward but
faithful coming home to you.
See us, Lord, coming up
the trail, on the snow-
covered mountain,
on our way
home.

snow

THE DEEPEST LOVE

> *"You shall love the Lord, your God, with all your heart, with all your being, with all your strength, and with all your mind...."*
>
> Luke 10:27

Envision a robust, mature black man being placed on a public block in a strange land and sold to the highest bidder like a beast of burden. A rigorously painful scene from our past? Yes. But there was something even more deplorable: this same man forced to see his wife and children publicly humiliated in the same cruel way. A strong man might bear his own shame with courage. But to see his loved ones degraded: who could bear that?

God the Father also watched a painful scene. He saw his divine Son suffer and die before a jeering mob. Nothing can speak to us more vividly of the depth of God's love for us than our heavenly Father's mercy— his willingness to permit the crucifixion of Jesus to redeem us from our sins, unworthy though we are.

How deep should be our love for him?

Father God, what can I do? What can I say? How can I summon up the adoration, obedience, and service that I want to offer to you? Fill me with your grace. Enfold me in your peace and power.

crucified

KNOWING MORE THAN KNOWLEDGE

"...so that people might seek God, even perhaps grope for him and find him, though indeed he is not far from any one of us.

Acts of the Apostles 17:27

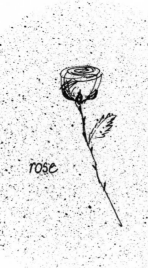

rose

Imagine for a moment that your father lived in a remote and inaccessible corner of the Himalayas and that he had been there since you were an infant. Your mother would undoubtedly try to describe him to you. She would try to bring him to life through words and pictures.

As a result, you would know certain facts about him, but you would not know him personally. Only if he were to visit you, so you could see him, hear him, and touch him, would you come to know him in a direct and personal way.

Most of us have difficulty relating to God, our Father, in a personal way. Preachers and teachers try to bring God to us through words and images, but sometimes words fail to engage our hearts.

God wants to be close to each one of us, but we tend to perceive him as remote—above and beyond our daily lives. If we are thoughtful and observant, if we look beneath the surface flux of our lives, we will see that God shines forth through his creation not as a faint shadow but as a personal, powerful, tender, and beneficent creator and sustainer of our lives.

We see him every day in the unique glory of the sunset; the soft loveliness of the rose; the timeless majesty of the redwood; the fleet, wild beauty of the deer; the universal warmth and tenderness of a mother's embrace; the awesome selflessness of a life risked to save another; and the quiet, loving presence of a faithful friend in a moment of deep need. God is living; God is everywhere. He shouts his divinity and love. It echoes throughout the universe.

Father God, I rejoice in your love. I marvel at your mercy.
I thank you, especially, for the men and women who
share my life. Give me, Lord, wisdom and light to see you
in the goodness that goes on all around me daily, in the
holiness that I frequently miss because of my fears and
preoccupations. Let me see you, Lord, in every creature
and every created thing.

CHAPARRAL

*To you, O Lord, I cry! for fire has
devoured the pastures of the plain, and flame
has enkindled all the trees of the field.*

Joel 1:19

Groves of chaparral, consisting of thorny shrubs
and small trees, cover much of the foothills of southern
California. During the hot summer months and dry
fall, these small shrubs and trees survive with little or
no rain. Fires occur frequently because of the arid
conditions.

These fires serve a peculiar regenerative purpose.
Seeds from the burnt chaparral fall to the ground and
are irrigated by winter rains. Later, new growth
emerges and bears beautiful desert flowers. The
bright flaming orange of these flowers is strangely
reminiscent of the destructive flames that made their
lives possible.

Most of us go through periods in our lives when we
are overcome for a while by our own weaknesses and
the assault of temptations. We may try to rationalize
our behavior, but in our hearts we know that we are
sinning. In moments of clarity, we realize our betrayal.
We burn with shame.

God knows that we want to escape our estrange-
ment from him. Mercifully, he sends his winter rains of
grace upon us to activate our seeds of faith. He calls us
out of our sins into a rich new growth of holiness under
his protection and power. We become, like the desert
flowers, beautiful in his sight.

*Holy Spirit, you send your light and truth throughout the
universe into every heart and mind. Thank you for your
loving call. We rejoice in your patience with those who
struggle to you out of their past, out of their mistakes,
ignorance, and sin. Save them. Lift them up. Lead them
into a virtue and goodness that is strong and enduring.*

CENTRAL CHARACTER

For God has put it into
their minds to carry out his purpose....

Revelation 17:17

The creations of human hands, however honest, primitive, or inspired, carry an artificial quality that is ineradicable. God the Creator is an artist who can be imitated but not equaled.

In the theater, set designers recognize this limitation. They focus on one aspect of the dramatic situation. They seize one aspect of a scene and develop an emphasis. It may be a blazing light or an overwhelming shadow, perhaps a strategically placed doorway through which a central character emerges at a critical point. Good set designs speak to us and create moods. They open our hearts to participating in the drama.

God has designed for each of us a life that is full of drama, moods, and meaning. We are role players but unique and self-directed. We create our roles, dialogue, and destiny within the eternal plan of the divine Playwright.

Our playscript may seem full of too many highs and lows. In our turbulent contemporary society, good and evil clamor for our attention. Heroes and villains confront us boldly. Victory and defeat emerge in widely varying patterns. God's plan for us is not melodrama, however. It is real. The fruit of our labors, the result of our decisions, are ours alone, binding and eternal.

Jesus, your role in carrying out the Father's plan leads, guides, and inspires me. You are the central character in my life, the light in my darkness, the path that I will follow.

DRAWING TOGETHER

*May [you] have strength to comprehend...what
is the breadth and length and height and depth,
and to know the love of Christ that surpasses
knowledge....*

Ephesians 3:18, 19

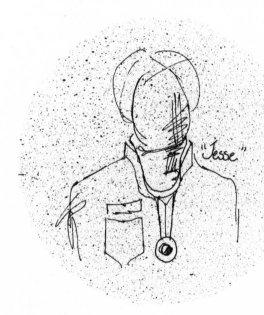

Jesse was a successful doctor—in many ways more than a doctor. As you came to know him, you became aware of his wide range of interests, his active imagination and sensitive intelligence. Jesse probed instinctively and provocatively into many intellectual targets of opportunity.

During my medical appointments, we would sometimes drift into discussion. I frequently took away from those sessions insights that widened my understanding and perceptions.

In a particularly personal and reflective moment, he told me about a trip he had taken to Oregon—a visit with his oldest daughter, someone he loved deeply but with whom he had never fully and successfully come to terms.

He said, "It was strangely fortuitous that shortly after my arrival we received a call from an ailing relative downstate. We drove along the breathtaking swath of the Oregon coast for hours—just the two of us. As we talked, our hearts opened to each other in a deep and unguarded way. It was a totally unforseen time of healing and drawing together."

He paused, then turned to me and said with great earnestness and simplicity, "God provides opportunities."

If you have given up on an elusive but worthy goal; if you have waited, seemingly in vain, for a reconciliation with someone you love; if your heart still clings to hope for a hopeless situation, remember Jesse, the doctor who was healed. Hear him recounting God's great gift of opportunity. Share with him the grace of trusting and the joy of fulfillment.

Loving God, your plan for my life is a joy and a mystery. How incomprehensible is your loving care and providence! Teach me patience, Lord. Give me the grace of waiting— obediently, expectantly, and joyfully—no matter how long the days and nights. Let my trust be in you and in your love.

A GLIMPSE OF GOD

How varied are your works, Lord!

Psalm 104:24

We stood on the beach at Tampa Bay in the morning sun expectantly waiting for the launching of the space shuttle. Suddenly, we could see, miles away, not the shuttle but its vapor trail. We were entranced by the distant sign of that rapidly rising spaceship.

God is like that. We see his effects—his vapor trail—his image in the things of earth, in people and places, in objects and events.

Some people identify the underlying presence of God surely and easily. Their expectant faith brings swift reward. Other people have narrowed their spiritual vision. They restrict God to the sanctuary, to private time, and to academic halls. They miss his daily pervasive presence and love.

Life is like a cosmic slide show. Images of the living God are repeatedly projected onto the screen of our daily lives. We can choose to see or to turn away, but the screening goes on. The images never cease coming. God's love surges continuously.

A ministry of love and compassion from caring people at the moment of dying may be our last and best image of God on earth. Yet some hearts remain hard even to the end. We can only pray that at the very end—the last split second—even the hardhearted can catch a glimpse of the reality behind the vapor trail—a glimpse of God, his love, and his forgiving mercy.

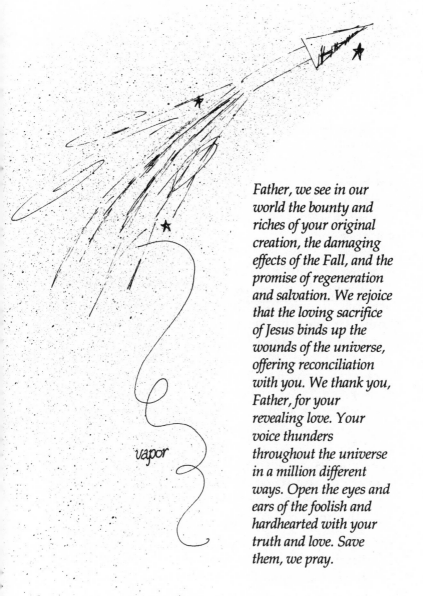

vapor

Father, we see in our world the bounty and riches of your original creation, the damaging effects of the Fall, and the promise of regeneration and salvation. We rejoice that the loving sacrifice of Jesus binds up the wounds of the universe, offering reconciliation with you. We thank you, Father, for your revealing love. Your voice thunders throughout the universe in a million different ways. Open the eyes and ears of the foolish and hardhearted with your truth and love. Save them, we pray.

UNIFIED IN WONDER

For a race blessed by the LORD are they and their offspring.

Isaiah 65:23

A sunset is like God's grace—unique in splendor, awesome in power, and available to everyone—the poor, the outcast, and the most humble. It is a universal gift.

The dramatic end of daylight can be enjoyed from a private vantage point, affording ample time for reflection. Or it can be viewed in the company of others, perhaps at the end of a daylong beach picnic or from the deck of a ship. Even in a group, a sunset can be a solitary experience, a time when no one comments, when everyone is simply full of looking.

I remember one December afternoon when my daughter Joanne called to us from the porch of our big white vacation house on the beach, "Come, see the sunset."

We drifted out in ones and twos and were soon unified in wonder at the unique splendor of a Florida sunset over the Gulf of Mexico. It was a powerful family experience that brought us together and held us there—together—on that little porch.

Like God's grace, that sunset brought a deep peace. We experienced a special intimacy from sharing that marvelous and stunning display of God's beauty. We lingered together, long after the sun had disappeared over the horizon.

Loving God, we thank you for our families, for placing each of us in the center of a compassionate heart of love, a heart in which our faults and sins can be understood and forgiven, where our wounds are bound up and healed in our commitment to you and to one another. I thank you, Father, that when I am alone I am able to draw on my family's strength and love—a love that is always there for me, that is part of me forever.

THE COMING OF SUMMER

*I am prompt, I do not hesitate
in keeping your commands.*

Psalm 119:60

I can vividly recall going to school on damp, cool mornings in the early spring. My mother, in her careful and protective way, made me wear a sweater or jacket. When I came home in the afternoon, the sun waxed hot, and it felt like early summer. My feet would become heavy as the unaccustomed heat slowed me down. I would sometimes strip off my sweater and drag it along with one hand while I lugged my book bag with the other.

My sluggish walk home from school has its counterpart in the spiritual life. After the primal energy of our conversion subsides, we have a tendency to slow down spiritually. Our past remains a problem. Our sinful preconversion attitudes and habits are not easily cast off. We find ourselves deferring full entry into our new spiritual life.

God understands our weaknesses and the difficulties of change. He sends his grace. He calls us to action. He beckons us to move on, to acclimate ourselves to the newly found warmth, vitality, and fire of his power and love in our hearts and minds. He invites us to savor the daily reality of intimacy with him. He calls us to an eternal summer of mutual love that is ever fresh, vital, and new.

*Lord, you have given me the precious gift of faith. I am
eternally grateful. Lift me out of my tepid mediocrity. Help
me to move on, to scale the spiritual heights to which you
call me. Hasten and strengthen my steps so that I can
remain by your side—close to you always.*

ON THE TRAIL

"I will protect you wherever you go...."
Genesis 28:15

I was alone in the church. Feeling tired and discouraged, I sat back in the pew, closed my eyes, and turned my mind and heart over to Jesus. In my reverie, I seemed to be with him on a dangerous mission of some kind. We were passing through enemy territory, going through a thick forest on a narrow, little-used trail. We could hear the enemy on every side and had to move quickly to outdistance them.

I tripped over a large root and twisted my ankle badly. It was obvious that I could no longer keep up. I felt panic; my heart pounded. Then I looked up and my eyes met the eyes of Jesus. I started to tell him to go on, but he darted back quickly, picked me up, tossed me across his shoulders, and moved ahead as swiftly and silently as before.

Coming out of my reverie, I felt refreshed and encouraged, affirmed and loved in a special way. I wanted to shout my feeling from the housetops—to share my experience of the deep love of Christ—a love that is there for each of us, for every living soul, on every trail, in every forest, no matter how remote, desolate, or forbidding.

Thank you, Jesus for not leaving me. Thank you for coming back for me again and again. Thank you, Lord, that I don't have to die—alone, friendless, and scared—on some lonely unmarked trail.

NOTHING BUT GOD

Moses went up the mountain to God.

Exodus 19:3

At some point in their lives many people hit bottom morally and spiritually. Only then do they look up and see God reaching down to them. They respond only when everything else has been taken away.

Most of the great saints did not need this kind of motivation. Early in their lives they divested themselves of worldly goods, honors, and attachments in order to depend totally and solely on God, to possess nothing but him.

There is a strange blessedness in having nothing but God, even for short periods. Being alone with God is a spiritual time of opportunity. In the rich, dynamic, and active silence of prayer and meditation, our love for God grows and deepens. We come to know that having nothing but God is having nothing but everything.

Jesus, Brother and Lord, Master and Savior, you are my light and my life. Grant me time to be alone with you. Lighten my daily burden of distractions and cares. Give me time on the mountaintop with you, where we can be alone together.

THE CHILDREN ON THE BEACH

...it is not the will of your heavenly Father that one of these little ones be lost.

Matthew 18:14

It was late July, sunny, cool, and dry—a perfect Montana day in the Rockies on the shores of Lake McDonald. We were at the south end of this magnificent, unspoiled body of water. Around us, forested mountains rose majestically in every direction. The view was breathtaking.

I was on the beach with my three grandchildren, ages two, five, and six. They played on the rocky shore. David, the littlest one, sat almost in the water, intent on examining the many multicolored stones. Occasionally stopping to toss a small pebble into the water, he was serenely happy and absorbed in his work.

The older boys, George and Matt, played warrior. Pieces of driftwood they had picked up served as guns and swords. They prowled among the larger rocks planning strategy and occasionally swooping down to raid the enemy on the shore.

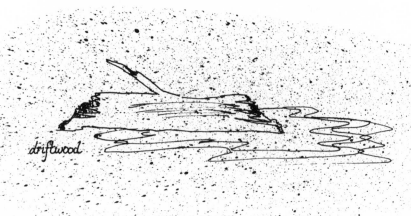

driftwood

Letting my imagination roam, I could see in my mind's eye three primitive children of an earlier age, the youngest naked, the other two wrapped in rough animal skins. They would undoubtedly have played on that beach in exactly the same way. There was a universality and a timelessness in that small tableau.

Was my role equally archetypal? The grandfather, the patriarch, watching over the children while the parents were busy hunting for food or gathering firewood. Would an old man of an ancient time see all the wonders of that awesome place as I did, as gifts of a good God? Would he utter in his heart a prayer of thanksgiving?

I'll never know, of course. But I feel a special kinship with him, a sharing of roles as proud sentinels with the same responsibilities, scarred veterans of a long life and witnesses of the same glory and splendor—of our beautiful grandchildren—in that mysterious and wonderful place.

Father God, your heart of love inspires and leads every Christian parent. Your care for your children is fiercely protective—stronger than armies, mightier than nations. We thank you that when we become tired, discouraged, or angry, we can look to your grace in us. Let your love, Father, flow through us to our children in power and wisdom and in mercy always.

LETTING GO

For you are great and do wondrous deeds;
and you alone are God.

Psalm 86:10

Too often our faith seems to be in our faith—not in God. Our spiritual life becomes self-obsessive. We are overwhelmed by our need to feel saved, to feel out of danger. These attitudes can close our minds to what God is saying to us.

Too many of us prefer to "say our prayers" rather than talk lovingly in a deeply personal way with our heavenly Father. Religious rites and practices are meant to lead us to the living God, but formalism and rigidity can turn them into sterile barriers or God-substitutes.

Fellowship, good works, and even worship can become drained of God's presence if we attempt to control and shape the power of religion in our lives in accordance with our personal convenience and biases.

God is the source of all our power. He calls us to his work in our homes and in our churches. He calls us to a radical Christian life—a life that seems foolish in the eyes of the world and inconvenient and upsetting to our self-obsessive and weak vision.

God calls us to constant change, to complete surrender and submission—on his terms. And he lovingly sends us more than adequate grace to strengthen and empower us, to draw us, and to keep us close to him and open to what he is saying to our inner hearts.

Jesus, I love only you and—through you—everyone.

WILDFLOWER

I waited, waited for the LORD;
who bent down and heard my cry....

Psalm 40:2

The driveway next door is solid concrete, six inches thick. It was built to sustain the weight of two-ton automobiles, and it does its job well. There are a few cracks here and there, but nothing major.

Toward the edge of the driveway near the street, I noticed a small sprig of green coming up through a crack in the concrete. It turned out by late spring to be a wildflower—deep blue. I marveled at the tenacity and stamina of that small plant.

Love is like that flower. Human love, even that of a small child, has the power of armies and of nations. The enduring, faithful love of a child, spouse, or friend can save, redeem, and regenerate hopeless, broken, and degenerate lives. Nothing is clearer in human life than the power of love and its ability to shine and grow stronger in adversity.

The love of Jesus for each of us is a shining victory, a glorious triumph, and a rescue operation of universal proportions. How tragic to see a man or a woman trapped in guilt and fear because of sin—not realizing that love and deliverance are close at hand. How unnecessary to die on the moral battlefield unaware that the war is over, the enemy defeated, and the tables being laid for the victory banquet.

Jesus saved you on Calvary. He watches you, and when he sees the sprig of your loyalty rising bravely through the concrete of your environment, he sends help —his love, his protection, and his empowering grace.

Jesus, your love for me is constant and shining, powerful and unremitting. It seeks me out at dawn and follows me through the day. Thank you, Lord, for caring, for remembering me. Give me the gift of confidence, spiritual stamina, and a constant and ready faith.

CHILDREN OF A LESSER GOOD

*"There is none like you and
there is no God but you...."*

2 Samuel 7:22

Picture in your mind's eye the hyperacquisitive man and woman. Observe how they respond to the naturally good things of earth with eagerness. Unfortunately, they sometimes mistake these natural pleasures and treasures for the whole of reality, for all that is. They become obsessed with material things, with worldly possessions, seeing these objects and experiences as ends in themselves. They become captive of the purely natural world, cut off from spiritual values and realities, from the possibility of a higher life. They live in a world of lesser goods.

God calls explicitly for our love and loyalty. He wants to be paramount, to be at the center of our lives. He never wearies of our obedience and reverence. He rejoices in our prayers and good works. He calls each man and woman to a unique intimacy with him. He calls us to an eternal life of goodness and holiness that begins now.

The choice is ours. If lesser goods become dominant in our lives, then they are lesser goods no more. They have become lesser gods who need to be rejected and turned out. God alone is God, and our true happiness is in him.

*Jesus, my life is full of the trivial but necessary. I am
hounded by the pressing but unimportant. I forget my real
self, who I am and who my Lord is. I become the busy,
empty creature of the day-to-day. Give me the grace, Lord,
to place you first in my life. Help me, Lord, to find regular
time for worship and praise. If I do not find you, Lord, find
me. Draw me to your heart.*

WONDERS TO SHARE

And I will work wonders in the heavens
and on the earth....

Joel 3:3

Bar Harbor, Maine, can be chillingly cold in summer. It certainly was that August day with the water temperature reading the same as the air temperature, about fifty-five degrees.

My seven little ones splashed along the shore with my wife and me, searching for shells and colorful stones. They were rewarded occasionally by the thrill of seeing a scampering sand crab.

We climbed up high among the rocks on one of the many points of land. It was quiet and still up there; even the children were hushed. We walked around a particularly large and interesting rock formation, and there, growing out of a crevice, was a single flower.

We all marveled at the vivid orange color and the delicate petals. The flower, apparently some kind of semi-Arctic species, seemed out of place in that inhospitable environment. Its beauty and delicacy were strangely enhanced by the rough, rocky setting. We were all fascinated by it and lingered awhile.

We could draw many messages of hope, courage, and divine providence out of that little flower and its brave, tiny world of survival. But I believe it was simply God, in his wisdom and love, giving us something startling and wonderful to share on that cold, windy, wonderful day at Bar Harbor many years ago.

Loving God, your eucharistic banquet table of love and
forgiveness draws our hearts together in an explosion of
gratitude and thanksgiving. Hear us. See our hearts.
Accept our love.

LIGHT OF HEAVEN

Give light to my eyes lest I sleep in death.

Psalm 13:4

What is more glittering and colorful, bright and attractive, than the finale of a Broadway musical? The audience is carried forward hypnotically by color, sound, and movement into a world of pleasing fantasy. But after the show, when the lights are down, the sets look drab and lifeless.

In our daily lives, first impressions frequently convey an appealing surface glitter, sometimes an exciting promise. But not every situation or person lives up to our expectations. Too often we experience disillusion and disappointment.

Knowing and experiencing God is a different process. In the beginning, God can appear forbidding. We may feel guilty, knowing that he is calling to us to turn from shallow and sinful pleasures that we may enjoy. God's call to goodness may seem dreary and restrictive. Negative and distorted Christian teaching can reinforce these false ideas.

To see through the sometimes drab and halfhearted presentation of Christian truth to the glorious freedom that Jesus brings can be difficult for some people—a long process of trial and error. A very few, like Paul on the Damascus road, are struck down suddenly by God's sovereign power. Their conversion is immediate.

Others instinctively recognize the strength, joy, and wisdom to be found in the Christian life. From their earliest years these men and women seem blessed in a special and mysterious way. Their eyes see through the false and shallow. They look beyond the lights of the city for something better, brighter, and eternal.

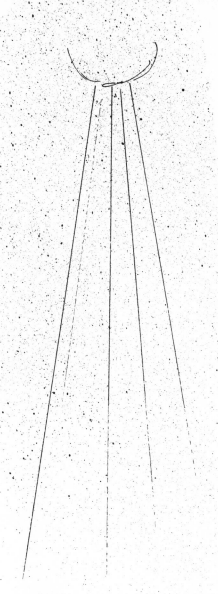

light

Holy Spirit, you are the light of heaven, the bond between the Father and the Son, the inspiration of our prayers, and the source of our best and highest aspirations. Give us the grace and wisdom to ever seek the Light, to rejoice in the dawn on arising, to know the sun at midday, to rest in the glory of the sunset, and to retain God's love and light in our hearts through the long nights.

THE LORD'S LOVE

*...in him we have put our hope [that] he will
also rescue us again....*

2 Corinthians 1:10

innocence

During prayer I came to a point of peace and silence, a time of reverie. I let my mind and heart roam.

I seemed to be traveling in a remote and arid place. Suddenly, in the distance I saw the body of a man lying on the roadside. Drawing closer, I was stunned to discover that it appeared to be my body lying there in that desolate and empty place.

Two men approached. Seemingly oblivious to my presence, they examined the body. One of them spoke out of obvious concern: "Poor guy, I wonder who he is, where he comes from?" The other said, "Let's take a look."

They searched every pocket but found only a small piece of notepaper. Upon it was written simply, "This child belongs to the Lord Jesus Christ." As one of the men read aloud this brief declaration, the body went through a series of progressive mutations, becoming visibly younger at each stage. Finally, it became the body of a young child, not more than three or four.

The two men stared at the note. One of them gently placed it on the body. Then they turned and left quickly.

I looked at the body of the child that was me, at the young face so full of innocence—an innocence I had lost in bits and pieces, that had somehow crumbled silently away. I licked my dry lips and tasted the sweetness of a child's faith.

I knelt down beside the body, bowed my head, and said a prayer for understanding. When I raised my head, the body was gone. I went on my way, conscious of my Lord's love in a new and deeper way.

Jesus, you alone know the depths of my needs and aspirations, the fervor with which I cling to my ideals and the shining hopes of my youth. You also know my pain— the burning shame I feel in falling—my angry stumbling as I flee my sins. Thank you, Jesus, for seeing my hand reaching out to you, for your healing and empowering grace—for being a Lord who brings resurrection of faith and new life to every open and contrite heart.

AN INSIDE STORY

*For the kingdom of God is not a matter of food
and drink, but of righteousness, peace, and joy
in the holy Spirit.*

Romans 14:17

Marty had been an apple grower for forty years. His orchards were well-known and successful. He should have been happy, but he wasn't.

"People have been brainwashed," he said. "They want apples that look like those things in the magazine pictures. All of our fruit—apples, peaches, plums—must have a certain look to sell. Taste and flavor doesn't count. Look at this apple. It's the most delicious I've ever grown, but it won't sell. It doesn't have the right look." He added with some irony, "I put these in the apple butter, and people wonder why it tastes so good."

Our society is preoccupied with appearances, with the way people look in magazines and on television. We have made a cult of the superficial. If it looks good, it must be good. Inner strength—character and conviction—are downplayed and frequently ignored. Books are written and lectures are given about having the right look, the look of success.

apple

Scripture says nothing about the physical appearance of Jesus. None of the great saints have been described in terms of their physical attributes. The inner fire of faith, moral courage, spiritual commitment, and loyalty to God are the distinguishing characteristics of holy men and women.

Most of what is really important in a

person's life goes on in the inner sanctum of the heart and mind. Jesus, in his teaching, made it abundantly clear that the kingdom of God is within us.

God cannot be charmed into approval of our lives. No one can beguile God. Salvation is a free gift of God, but it does not come cheaply. It is freely given on God's part, but the cost to us can be great. The cost is change—a deep inner radicalization—a new life in which the superficial, the glossy, and the short-term are set aside, sometimes painfully and with great difficulty, for deeper, more enduring values.

But the rewards are great. What would a man or woman exchange for the inner peace of knowing and loving Jesus?

Holy Spirit, you see our inner hearts, our real selves. You know us as we are. Help us to strip away our superficial obsessions. Give us the grace to see ourselves clearly. Create in us a strong faith and an inner peace so we can become and remain our best and true selves, naked and unafraid, now and forever.

THROUGH HEARING

Thus faith comes from what is heard, and what is heard comes through the word of Christ.

Romans 10:17

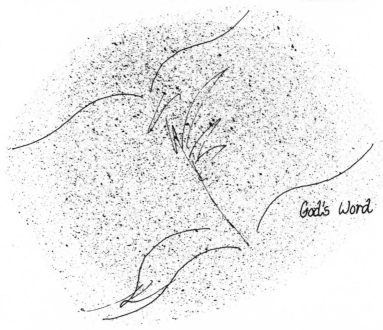

God's Word

Bill came into the Lord. He received a conversion experience and turned his life over to Jesus. He entered the Church. He had heard the call of God clearly.

But Bill's faith has not grown. He has become a spiritual minimalist. His religious life is at the lowest common denominator. His low-risk morality is feeble and self-centered, and his faith is dim and dying.

Many Christians are like Bill. They begin with enthusiasm but fail to fully grasp the essential realities of the spiritual life. They perceive being in the state of grace as simply being free from sin. They miss the deeper meaning—the real substance of grace—which is sharing in the divine life. They fail to experience grace as a dynamic, active, personal friendship with God.

Because of media distortion of reality and half-hearted Christian preaching and teaching, many people miss the completeness of spiritual truth. They fall short of the fullness of knowledge and action that God intends for them.

They see peace as the absence of war rather than as a condition of active justice and love among men and women. They perceive abortion as a woman's choice, failing to see the lack of choice for the unborn child whose life is at stake. They view a religious retreat as a flight from the world rather than as a dynamic and personal meeting with Jesus. Their faith seeps away as they seek the minimum in submission to God and the easy way out of moral challenges. They waffle. They begin to accept half-truths and lies.

God calls out to each of us—day and night. He wants us to see and hear the fullness of his truth. He wants to draw us to genuine holiness. If we listen to his voice, if we respond to his grace and inspiration, we will be drawn closer and closer to him. We will begin truly to understand his words and the full beauty, excellence, and dignity of the life to which he is calling each of us.

God, you spoke your word. You sent your Son to redeem us. You inspired the writers of the holy Scriptures. You send your grace upon us and your truth into our hearts. We thank you, Father. We pray that we may always hear the undiluted fullness of your word. Give us your light and power so that we may become and remain holy—fully informed, fully aware, and faithful to your call.

THE MOUNTAIN

"...the LORD will be passing by."

1 Kings 19:11

It was a bright day in early June over forty years ago. Mary Dodd was five years old at the time. Railroad tracks ran right through the center of our small community. Downtown, just beyond the station, there were several switches. Mary had somehow wandered away from her parents and gotten into the control-switch area. As I stood on the station platform, I wondered what she was doing out there all by herself.

Suddenly, two things became painfully clear to the small group gathered with me on the platform. One, Mary had her foot jammed in one of the switches. Two, a train, already visible, was bearing down on her.

I wanted to move but couldn't. Paralyzed with fear, I could only stare in mute horror. Everyone else seemed to be in the same helpless condition.

Then, seemingly from out of nowhere, a huge, rangy man appeared. He sprinted to the switch and carefully but swiftly slipped Mary's foot from her shoe. He carried her to the platform and placed her down gently just as the train roared by.

Everyone, including her relieved and jubilant parents, crowded around Mary. After a moment, I looked up and saw in the distance the girl's rescuer loping along in strong, powerful strides. He was, strangely enough, running away from the scene of his heroics. We never found out who he was. No one had ever seen or heard of him before. He must have been just passing through our little town.

As I gazed at his retreating form, I thought, *He was, in the critical moment of his heroic act, truly another Christ.* I hoped that he knew it and was simply fleeing human gratitude, that in his running, he was running to the Lord.

Jesus, your example of heroic, unselfish love looms before us like a mountain we cannot climb. Thank you, Lord, for the messengers you send, heroic men and women who act out your love in our lives, who show us the possible, who call us forward to patient, hopeful climbing, who direct our eyes and hearts to the summit.

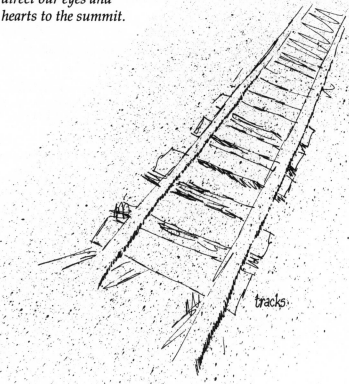

tracks

ENDURING BEAUTY

Charm and beauty delight the eye....

Sirach 40:22

Copper objects are lustrous, warm, and attractive, but they tend to oxidize readily and lose their initial beauty. If we add tin and a little lead to copper, we produce bronze, which does not oxidize as quickly. Therefore, it has a more enduring beauty.

Like the beauty of copper, the religious faith of some men and women does not endure. It can become corroded with pride, disobedience, and disloyalty to God and his Church. Sometimes it is damaged or destroyed by a lack of understanding and love on the part of Church officials and leaders. For a variety of reasons, men and women become alienated from God and his Church.

In their spiritual isolation, ex-Christians have a serious practical problem. They have to deal with their personal and moral values and beliefs. Some return to the Christian community. Others try to live a spiritual life without God and his Church.

teakettle

Their unaided efforts usually fail quickly in a world dominated by unbridled competition, conflict, and self-seeking. They experience disappointment, anger, and resentment when their associates reject their noble aspirations and values. This lack of support and rejection can turn these former Christians to deep bitterness. Like oxidizing copper, they lose their warm and shiny glow.

God has supreme understanding and compassion. He calls everyone to surrender to his love and to membership in the Body of Christ, his Church. He graciously sends his grace into every surrendered heart, creating a spiritual alloy that can resist the corrosive effect of any disappointment or failure. When our goals, our work, and our rewards are from God, no human action, no worldly rebuff or unforeseen event, can ever crush us completely.

God wants to create in each of us a spiritual glow that will endure and attract others to his forgiveness, protection, and empowering love.

Jesus, many of your brothers and sisters seek goodness in the wrong places. They act in misguided idealism, confused about moral and spiritual values. Dear Lord, please reveal yourself to them in power, let them see the true glory of your Church, take them by the spiritual hand, lead them to the light that will satisfy their hearts and fill their minds with lasting peace and a joy that endures.

eyes

THE EYES OF CHRIST

*[Your adornment is] the hidden character of
the heart...which is precious in the sight
of God.*

1 Peter 3:4

Children grow in confidence and moral courage
when the spiritual soil of their surroundings is rich and
fertile and the rain of God's grace and guidance is
plenteous and gentle. Parents, pastors, and friends can
supplement God's gentle rain of grace. They can affirm,
encourage, and bless children with eyes of love, eyes
that care and persist in caring.

Jesus offers each man, woman, and child the ultimate invitation to spiritual growth. He offers each of us
his unconditional forgiveness, mercy, and grace. There
is nothing more we need in order to attain power-filled
and spiritually victorious lives. His are the supreme,
caring eyes of love.

How often have we turned away from the loving
eyes of Jesus? How often have we not responded to the
innocence and purity of the burning eyes of Christ?

A mother and father correcting a child will say,
"Look at me when I speak to you." The parent knows
the core of communication is in the eye and the heart.
Jesus says to each of us, "Look at me—look into my eyes
of love."

Jesus wants you to strip away every veil of shame,
fear, and deception. He wants your innocence and
purity. Jesus wants to see himself in your eyes of love.

*Dear Jesus, I raise my head to the heavens, my eyes to your
glory, and my heart to your love.*

DAWNING LIGHT

...we possess the prophetic message that is altogether reliable. You will do well to be attentive to it, as to a lamp shining in a dark place, until day dawns and the morning star rises in your hearts.

2 Peter 1:19

chair

Imagine yourself being brought into a dark room. You are led to a chair in the center of the room and seated. A small dim light is switched on next to you. In the limited glow, you can see only the chair you are in and the end table next to it.

In a few minutes the light is turned up slightly, and you can see a bit more. The room seems attractive and well-furnished. The light is increased in intensity several times. Each time you see more of the room. Finally, you see it in full light. You are surprised that the furnishings now look soiled and worn and that there are piles of waste in the corners of the room.

Our lives are like that. We harbor sin in our hearts but remain blind to its presence and its power over us. We rationalize. We evade ugly truths about ourselves.

God knows our weaknesses. He sends the light of self-knowledge into our darkness, just a little at a time. He wants to gently bring us to a full realization of our disobedience and ingratitude. He doesn't overwhelm us all at once with a full revelation of our moral and spiritual failings.

Through God's generosity and mercy, we come slowly to the light of self-knowledge. Through the power of his grace, we are able to radically change our direction, to reverse our course. We are able to see clearly and act decisively, to restore and renew our spirits. We are able to live the life that God intended for us from the beginning.

Give me, dear Jesus, self-knowledge, realism, and humility. Help me daily to rebuild and strengthen my heart in your image. Give me light and power of your Holy Spirit.

RUNNING TOGETHER

May the Lord direct your hearts to the love of God and to the endurance of Christ.

2 Thessalonians 3:5

football

A football player returning a kickoff runs the gauntlet of opposing players. They converge on him with ferocity—twisting, straining, grasping, sometimes launching themselves like projectiles at his elusive, evasive, and speedy form.

Going through our daily lives can frequently seem like a kickoff return. We encounter a continuing variety of challenges, temptations, and dangers. Each area of our lives offers its own special hazards.

Despite our deep love for one another, the often complex and tense intimacy of our family lives can severely test our ability to be patient, fair, and just. Gentleness and self-control can sometimes seem beyond our ability.

In our work situations, a climate of moral ambiguity and pragmatism can weaken our spiritual sensitivities, even on occasion our deepest convictions. Peer pressure is powerful.

In social settings, the moral climate can change suddenly. Conversations can move in directions we do not anticipate. We may have difficulty standing our moral ground.

Perhaps the most stressing challenges are experienced in deeply personal encounters. In these intimate moments, we may have problems in ascertaining right from wrong because of fluctuating emotional forces or long-established, self-destructive habits.

We are clearly at risk in each of these situations. We are running the spiritual gauntlet. We need to remember that each of us has a powerful inner resource. We have God's grace, the divine life, coursing within us.

We need to listen. God continually speaks to our hearts, particularly of the life and example of Jesus. In every situation, no matter how threatening or difficult, Jesus is with us. His example is clear. His promises are reliable. His strength is ours. He runs the gauntlet with us.

Jesus, you are the Father's gift, my model and my guide. Help me. Inspire me to follow your example of loving and caring with strength and courage no matter what the risk or cost. Live in my heart.

mimosa tree

PATTERNS

...God called out to him from the bush....
Exodus 3:4

I sat in Dennis' backyard, sipping tea and munching toast, content to be part of the morning scene. In the quiet, my ears caught the faint buzzing of bees. Several birds sang in a low key as if reluctant to break the peace. My eyes swept the yard.

Along the fence, a mimosa tree, a large hydrangea, and a rosebush thrived. Each had a profusion of flowers scattered in a random pattern against a green background of leaves and branches. Each of these patterns was different and appealing in a simple but unique way.

God scatters talents, aptitudes, and graces in each heart and mind. Through our actions, we weave these gifts into a special, personal pattern. God sees that each personality has its own distinctive flavor, and he uses us in unique and distinctive missions, callings, and vocations.

We can abort God's purpose in us if we hoard our gifts, if we fail to recognize, use, and appreciate them. Only if we act boldly and in faith can we become what God intended us to be from the beginning—uniquely beautiful in his sight and powerfully useful in his plan.

Father, you created us in singularity and multiplicity. You fashioned the mystery of our humanity. You bless our growth as complex personalities. Your hand and eye rest on each heart with love and tenderness. Thank you, Father, for the deep knowledge, the soul-satisfying understanding and consolation and joy of knowing that whatever our pain, suffering, or fear, we are not alone or unknown.

DESERT WALK

The LORD calls you back,
like a wife forsaken and grieved in spirit,
A wife married in youth and then cast off,
says your God.
For a brief moment I abandoned you,
but with great tenderness
I will take you back.

Isaiah 54:6-7

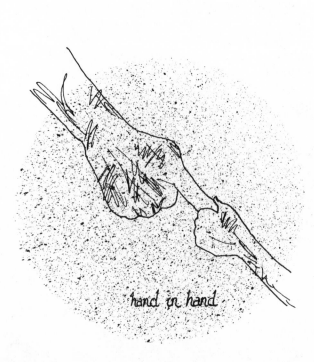

hand in hand

In prayerful reverie, I saw myself as a small child walking hand in hand with Jesus. We were crossing a desert. Jesus' large brown hand was holding my small hand firmly, and occasionally he smiled down at me. I felt happy just to be with him.

In late afternoon we arrived at the gate of a small village. Jesus said, "Wait here. I'll come back for you." I sat down among several small groups of people gathered just inside the gate.

It soon grew dark, and everyone drifted away. I was alone, and it was turning cold. I shivered. At every sound, I anxiously looked for the face of Jesus, but all I saw were the furtive glances of a few passing strangers.

I felt lost and abandoned and increasingly insecure. Then I remembered the words of Jesus. Suddenly, in a bright instant, I knew that Jesus would do exactly as he had said. I felt a deep peace. Shortly thereafter, I saw his dim but luminous figure coming toward me in the darkness.

The sincere, committed Christian spends a great deal of time in prayer—walking with Jesus, experiencing his love, enjoying the intimacy of fellowship.

Yet there are times when our fellowship with Jesus falters. We forget to keep the words of Jesus alive in our hearts. We neglect our friendship with our Lord.

Jesus respects our freedom. He doesn't interject himself roughly into our lives. He speaks gently in the inner forum of our hearts. If we are obedient and attentive, if we are listening, we will hear the sure word that Jesus loves us and that he will do exactly as he said— that he will come again in glory and take us home with him to his Father's house.

Lord God, your love endures forever. Your mercy is infinite. I rejoice in the mystery of your love for me. I do not know or understand why you care for me, but I find joy and fulfillment in your words of love and your promise of salvation.

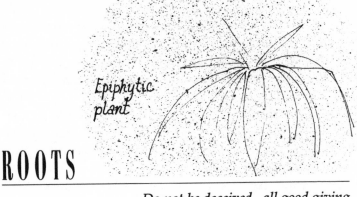

Epiphytic plant

ROOTS

Do not be deceived...all good giving and every perfect gift is from above....

James 1:16-17

Epiphytic plants stand on their heads. They live upside down. Their roots are in the air, and they take their nutrients from the atmosphere rather than the soil. They are oddities in the plant world, plants with a different perspective.

In Scripture, Saint Paul speaks to us frequently about spiritual threats and dangers—about the powerful downdraft of sins of the flesh and what results from the love of money. He points us to a higher life, a life of spiritual vision, sacrificial love, and personal holiness.

If we follow the Apostle's teaching, we will live upside down in the eyes of the world. We will be counterculture people, taking our spiritual nutrients, our guidance, and our direction from above.

We are free agents. We can reach up or down for our destiny. If what we permit to come into our hearts and minds is from above, it will lift us up, empower us, and draw us away from what is selfish, passing, and corruptible. We are oddities in the world, a people with roots in the heavens from whence our glory comes.

Sharpen our spiritual perspective, Lord. Give us the grace to see rightly and clearly, power to pierce the murky haze of media distortion. Strengthen us to stand apart and draw others to what is pure and holy—to the spiritual nutrients and power that come from and lead back to you.

A SHOUTING HEART

Give ear, listen humbly, for the LORD speaks.

Jeremiah 13:15

As part of a voluntary goodwill program for foreign visitors, we occasionally had people come to our home. It was an opportunity to offer Christian love, and we felt it would be edifying and informative for our seven children, who were then all quite young.

One of our most memorable visitors was Mr. Tanaka from Kyoto, Japan. He spoke no English, but he was accompanied by a young Japanese-American student who served as an interpreter. The conversation through this intermediary was surprisingly swift and easy.

Mr. Tanaka, a bright, amiable middle-aged man, was the owner of a large television station. To our delight, we found that he also had seven children. After a nice dinner, he was totally relaxed and at home. His primary interest was in our children—what they were doing and what they were thinking.

The children were shy with him at first, but soon everyone was talking and laughing and having a great time. The interests and activities of children in Japan fascinated us. We were having such a good time that the evening ran quite late.

Mr. Tanaka presented us with little gifts as he left, and I was pleased to see the gleam in his eyes as well as a few tears. It was a fine moment, exactly what the program was intended to accomplish.

Mr. Tanaka knew not one word of English, but his heart shouted love and we heard him.

Father God, I thank you for creation; for men, women, and children; for the sounds of speaking, singing, and shouting. For the vital surge of love engulfs the world through the hearts of ordinary people. When the politics of fear and hatred rage most fiercely, give us the grace and wisdom to act—to respond in love—in every way open to us.

GOLDEN TRIANGLE

*Herod and Pilate became friends that very day,
even though they had been enemies formerly.*

Luke 23:12

The Irish Claddagh ring is an interesting design. Two hands come together, each holding up one side of a heart. A crown rests on the heart. It is a charming and apt image of friendship—of two people uniting from the heart.

Friendship is a precious human value, but not all friendships are noble. Many enduring friendships are based on negative and immoral factors. Many involve common hatreds, dislikes, prejudices. Some involve the sharing of illicit pleasures. Others arise from gaining wealth by illegal means.

These unworthy friendships are real. They can involve commitment, even sacrifice, and they can last for long periods of time.

Genuine, loving, Christian friendships are triangular. They involve you, your friend, and God. God is first and fundamental. He is the source of our power and goodness. If we have surrendered our hearts to him, he undergrids, strengthens, and purifies everything we do, alone or with others. Without God at the center, our relationships never realize their fullness. Within his power, our friendships grow into strong, enduring Christian love.

God's grace is twofold. It enables us to integrate and strengthen our personal lives, and it binds us to one another in caring, sharing, and upbuilding ways. In the final analysis, Christian friendship is following an example—being Christ to one another.

Help me, Father God, to go beyond mutual and self-interest in my friendships. Give me your power in loving others. Help me to realize fully my desire to share my life with others. Let your heart fill mine in the painful moments of my inability to love.

OPEN BOOK

*Indeed, the word of God is living and
effective....*

Hebrews 4:12

The Bible is not an original document. It is a translation from ancient Aramaic and Greek texts. Through the centuries, our accumulated knowledge has enabled us to produce newer and more useful translations of God's word.

Today translations of the Bible are a valuable tool in worldwide evangelization. Brave and dedicated men and women spend a major share of their lives translating the Bible into primitive languages in jungles and other remote areas of the world.

Yet many of us overlook what may be the most important translation of the Bible. We forget that everyone doesn't read holy Scripture. For those who are unfamiliar with God's word, we, as Christians, may be the only Bible they will ever read. Our spirituality and how we act, talk, and conduct ourselves will be the official translation of the Bible to these men and women.

As a Christian, you know that every day of your life has the potential to become a glowing page of Scripture. If you are completely submitted to God's will and his authority over your life, if you manifest his love and compassion to others, your life will be an open book of a special kind.

Father God, I have been taught your word from my youth. Your truth has taken root in my heart and mind. I have been privileged to see your saints alive. Help me, Father, to speak and act out my inner convictions in the marketplace. Help me, in difficult situations, to be firm and clear and even heroic when that is needed. Let me never forget that your grace carries me, lights my way, and strengthens my heart.

MORNING LIGHT

At dusk weeping comes for the night;
but at dawn there is rejoicing.

Psalm 30:6

Many desert plants are covered with spikes and hooked outgrowths that appear hostile and intimidating. However, these stark and forbidding plants often bloom with surprising beauty.

At the foot of a palm tree outside our vacation cottage in southern Arizona, I noticed a number of delicate purple flowers on one of these desert plants. One evening when we returned from a day of sightseeing, the blooms seemed to have disappeared. Taking a closer look, however, I saw that they had simply closed up for the night. In the morning they would again open to greet the rising sun.

In the marketplace, in the world, we are besieged by darkness, by the night forces of evil, by pleasant-appearing temptations and sweet-sounding invitations to sin. Unwittingly, many of us open our hearts to these subtle and devastating influences. We absorb ideas and images that distort and destroy our inherent taste for goodness.

The wise Christian closes his or her heart to evil, immorality, and sin, to invitations to disobey and to be disloyal to a generous, good, and loving Father. The wise Christian opens his or her heart to the morning light of God's truth and love, to Jesus' loving call to spiritual joy, to the fruit of his promises, and to intimacy with the heart of our Savior.

Give us grace, Lord, to discern your will and purpose in every situation, especially in the shadows and the dark. Help us to move forcefully, with moral courage, in the dimness that often besets us. Help us to grasp and retain the light of your truth as our only standard, as our one sure guide and protection.

TIGER ON THE PATIO

Come, therefore, let us enjoy the good things
that are real, and use the freshness
of creation avidly.

Wisdom 2:6

Tiger, tiger, burning bright
In the forests of the night,
What immortal hand or eye
Could frame thy fearful symmetry?

William Blake
Songs of Experience

The walls around our patio are of untreated cypress. The rain, wind, and sun have weathered these boards in a fascinating way, creating in them a rich, varied texture.

When the sun or shadows move across the wood, the effect can be strangely pleasing. A unique quality—a beauty—is created that is difficult to describe. Words such as *honest*, *real*, and *primitive* come to mind, but none of them quite convey the experience.

God's work is designed for our delight. He places in our hearts a consonance with creation. I see those pristine cypress boards surrounding our patio as a special blessing from the Lord of heaven and earth. Like William Blake's shining tiger they speak to me of my God, and I rejoice, even with awe, knowing the loving hand and eye of the God who has blessed me.

Father God, you have entrusted to us our souls and the earth. Give us the grace to act boldly in protecting both our spirits and our physical environment from distortion and destruction. Help us, Lord, to maintain the holiness and purity of our hearts and the beauty and fruitfulness of the earth.

ANCHORED CABLES

...he may grant you in accord with the riches of his glory to be strengthened with power through his Spirit in the inner self....

Ephesians 3:16

The strength of heavy steel wires is multiplied many times over when they are intertwined to form cables. The process is serious technology. If the wires are not artfully and carefully shaped together in just the right way, the intertwined cable will lack integrity. It will snarl and twist out of shape under stress.

Families, churches, and communities, all men and women working together in common enterprises, face problems in human relationships. It is difficult to work together and to love and serve one another in changing, complex, and stressful situations. Unless there is a concentrated effort, a voluntary standing together, and unless the effort comes from deep within each member, the unified body will snarl and twist and sometimes come apart under pressure.

Saint Paul speaks frequently about the importance of unity; about the vine and the branches; about being one loaf; and most dramatically, about our being one Body in Christ.

Steel wires are shaped by exterior forces—by heat and pressure—and are brought into physical submission. Men and women are best shaped from within, through the attractive allurement of God's love and grace working in the interior life of each soul.

Men and women transformed by grace share in the divine life. They are able to serve one another with the mind and heart of Jesus, creating a unity that faintly but powerfully reflects the inner life of God.

cable

Holy Spirit, I want to love and serve the people you send to me in a strong and powerful way. Yet it so frequently seems beyond me. Personal fears, anxieties, and insecurities too often dominate my thoughts and actions. Give me your help, strength, and love. Extend my light and vision. Teach me to care for and nurture, to share with and listen to, and to pray daily for those whose lives are intertwined with mine. May my family, Church, and community become strong cables of God, bridges to eternity, anchored securely both in heaven and on earth.

A WAY OF TEACHING

Draw near to God, and he will
draw near to you.

James 4:8

Childhood memories strongly shape and form our hearts. Can you recall as a small child jumping into the front seat of your family car and sliding over to sit close to your dad? Perhaps you remember looking up into his face and feeling his arm slide protectively around you, snuggling you in a comfortable way.

Can you recall coming in from the yard with barely repressed tears—hurting from a fall, with skinned knees and a bruise on your cheek? Can you remember the peace of being enfolded in your mom's healing arms of love?

God prepares us for life. He schools our minds and hearts. He teaches us through these early childhood experiences a readiness to relate to him lovingly and freely in response to his generous and ever-present grace. It is beautiful and comforting to visualize our relationship to God in simple, real, and powerful ways —like drawing close to our dad in the old family car or drawing close to our mom in her healing arms of love.

Dear God, I know that you are far above me, that you live in unapproachable light, that your ways are not my ways. Yet I feel your deeply personal love and your presence in my quiet times of prayer. I praise and thank you. I rejoice in the openness, beauty, and tenderness of your Father-heart and your Mother-heart.

LEVEL GROUND

He came and preached peace to you who were
far off and peace to those who were near,
for through him we...
have access in one Spirit to the Father.

Ephesians 2:17-18

The crucifixion is a riveting scene; it can sear the soul. To see perfect Goodness disgraced and ridiculed because of our sins can make us feel worthless. Knowing our own sins so well, we may feel deeply discouraged.

We have to recall the message of Scripture that we are all equally called and equally loved by our crucified Savior. In the loving democracy of God, sincerity of heart is the only credential. It's always level ground before the cross.

We might perceive that ground to be very low to admit all repentant sinners. If so, we would be mistaken. The men and women who are figuratively gathered on Golgotha have been lifted up by their surrender to Jesus. They are on the broad and high plateau of the children of God.

Some are close to the cross, standing there defiantly, unafraid of the Roman soldiers and the jeering crowd. Others are filled with compassion but hesitant and fearful. They move timorously around the edges of the crowd.

Jesus sees and loves us all in our weaknesses and strengths but most of all in our friendship, in our being there, in our standing by, in our fidelity to him and to our brothers and sisters who stand with us—on the level ground before the cross.

Jesus, you stand by me in every trial and joy, on every peak and in every valley. Your loyalty and love exceed my vision and carry me beyond my hopes. Give me the grace, Lord, to be a brother and a sister to you—a friend, incorruptible in love.

A SINGULAR MIRACLE

Then Peter proceeded to speak and said, "In truth, I see that God shows no partiality."

Acts of the Apostles 10:34

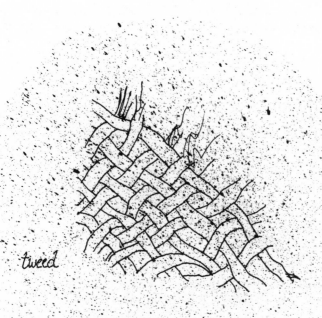

tweed

In a small shop in Dublin called the Weaver's Shed, beautiful tweeds are lovingly produced in a wide variety of colors and patterns. No more than thirty yards of a particular design is created. Whatever you buy is virtually exclusive.

God makes each man and woman as an exclusive creation, a singular miracle. Scripture tells us that God shows no favoritism or partiality. Each person is created to be a full and unique son or daughter of the Father.

How hard it is to heed this teaching in our struggle for survival and success. We draw close to amusing, clever, and accomplished people. Unattractive and unpopular people embarrass us. We judge on the basis of surface appeal and worldly stands of excellence.

God calls us to take a deeper look; to see the inner heart; to savor character, moral courage, and holiness. He wants to draw his people together to form a Body of Christ. In seeking true values in our friendships and in helping others, we will experience an unexpected blessing—more love, strength, and encouragement than we have given.

At our best, we can lift others up. Each person, without exception, is a supreme work of the Master. Each one has a claim on our concern, interest, and support. Our acceptance, love, and help can bring them hope that may be sorely needed. Our acts of love, however small or simple, can begin a miracle anew.

Father, we are all sinners, each of us weak, willful, and disobedient. Give us grace to see our faults and strength to overcome them. Provide us with vision and the will to help others so that we may all be what you wanted us to be—from the beginning.

MYSTERY

Children are transfixed with awe at the skill of a
magician. They marvel at the seemingly impossible
tricks he performs. Later they discover that it's all done
with mirrors, but that doesn't seem to destroy their
delight in mystery. Perhaps they sense what many
adults fail to understand—that most of our universe is
shrouded in mystery rather than captured in knowledge.

Christian civilization has been to some degree a
process of demystification of pagan fables and elimina-
tion of superstition and ignorance.

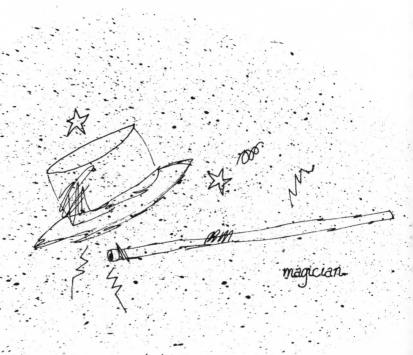

magician

This has sharpened our vision; unfortunately, some of us have become casualties of that experience. Many people are lured by a hope of eliminating all mystery in the universe. They seem unaware that as we discover new knowledge we unearth deeper mysteries of greater complexity and number. Mystery appears to be a continuing and important part of human experience.

The great Christian mysteries—the Creation, the Incarnation, the Resurrection—are unique. They are divinely revealed truth, designed to draw us forward and delight our hearts. They are not impenetrable. They can be partially understood by both reason and faith, and they grow in beauty and meaning for those who commit their lives to Jesus in prayer and good works.

The Scripture teaching that we must become as little children to enter the kingdom of heaven is not surprising. Perhaps the openness and honesty of a child's heart can penetrate mystery more sharply than the rigid agendas of scholars and researchers. If we truly open our minds to an innocent and full vision of reality, we will discover a surprising paradox—as our knowledge, understanding, and maturity increase, so will our appreciation of mystery also grow.

Jesus, your creation speaks to our hearts. Whether we hear you in the booming of thunder or the cooing of a dove, your call is distinctive and clear. Your voice in our hearts is personal and tender—like a kiss. The mystery of your love is beyond our senses and our full knowing but not beyond our grasp.

QUIET HOUSE

The whole earth rests peacefully,
song breaks forth....

Isaiah 14:7

Saturday morning I awoke early, went down to the kitchen, then retreated to our den with a cup of tea and a slice of toast. Through the window I could see our garden—a peaceful morning scene. My big old comfortable chair made staying awake difficult.

In a half-awake half-asleep reverie, my thoughts turned to my wife and children—silent witnesses to my morning vigil in our quiet house. I thought about them in their beds—innocent, immobile, and vulnerable. I felt like a caretaker of precious cargo, a watchman over jewels.

Sleeping is something only God could have thought of and created. It makes us all children again. It is so endearing. Even difficult and troubled people look innocent and peaceful on their pillows.

I felt God's peace that morning in a special way. I rested in it, knowing that the noise of Saturday family life would soon erupt. I knew that God created that, too—the special blessing of hearing my wife and children busily entering the day—putting the night behind them—together—on a late Saturday morning in our quiet house.

Loving God, your protection quiets my fears; your love stills my heart; your promise of salvation brings me peace. Thank you for your blessings. Thank you for the power of the Holy Spirit in our family life. It moves like a breeze through wind chimes—bringing us alive, awakening our music, opening our hearts to you and to one another.

tea

embrace

EARLY MORNING KISS

Is he not your father who created you?

Deuteronomy 32:6

Anthropologists tell us that the handshake originated among primitive men and women as a sign of peace. It was a simple outstretching of the hand and arm to indicate "No weapon, no threat."

We use many signs and overtures to convey warmth, acceptance, and affection. A smile, a look, a touch on the arm, an embrace, all communicate recognition and sometimes caring and love. These acts are universal spiritual connections that break down barriers between men and women. They unite and heal.

Uniting with God and receiving his healing power is an even more important spiritual act. A fruitful Christian way to begin each day is to make a morning offering to God: a loving expression of sorrow for our sins and a firm intention of changing our behavior, of being better, stronger witnesses of the gospel. This simple act of love and surrender can obliterate every trace of sin and failure. It will bring you closer to God, who forgives and remembers your sins no more.

Your heart in morning prayer can be like the heart of a child who bursts into the parents' bedroom in the early dawn, leaping joyfully into the arms of mother and father for an early morning kiss.

Your contrition and love can be an early morning leap into God's arms. If your heart is open and expectant, his kiss of love will be there for you.

Father God, my heart throbs with a powerful need for loving and being loved. You, Father, are the beginning and end of my life. Accept my weak but warm human love. See me, your child, reaching out to you.

LIVING WATERS

Streams of the river gladden the city of God,
the holy dwelling of the Most High.

Psalm 46:5

Our conference in Denver ended late on a Friday afternoon. Since I couldn't get a plane until Sunday, I scheduled a bus tour for Saturday morning. The weather was perfect, the air clear and dry. As we drove up into the mountains, I was impressed by the beauty of a turbulent roadside stream. The sunlight danced on the surface of the crystal-clear water.

When I commented on how cool and delicious the stream looked, the bus driver informed me that in spite of its inviting appearance, the stream was contaminated with chemicals from mining operations. That cool, beautiful stream was poisoned! I was surprised and disappointed.

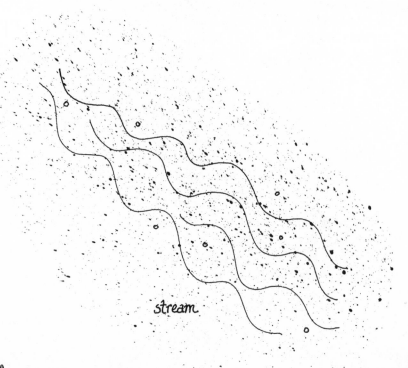

stream

We drove for a long while, all the way up to the Continental Divide. There, in the forest, we found spring water that was pure and drinkable.

God's grace is like that spring high in the mountains. It is always there for us. It is waiting to be found. When we seek God, when we pray and participate in the worship life of the Church, our hearts receive the pure, cool, living waters of God. But when we go into the world, things are different. We frequently encounter a poisonous lack of truth, honesty, and integrity. We realize we are operating amid moral hazards.

Not all of us are clever and shrewd; perhaps we are not exceptionally intelligent or highly educated. We may not be able to vanquish evil through clever argumentation or superior knowledge. We may have to rely on our faith and innocence.

Our integrity can sometimes serve as an eloquent judgment on unbelievers. Their hearts can be convicted of sin through the power and sincerity of the personal holiness we carry with us. We can all be honest, humble, and compassionate—that is within our power. And that small limited power of ours can be used by God in ways far beyond comprehension.

Lord God, your power runs in and through us. We are your channels and a source of life for others. Give us the grace to remain open, pure, and innocent. Help us to manifest a clear and bright integrity that will draw confused and angry hearts to you and your living waters of healing, unconditional love.

A HUMBLE AND CONTRITE HEART

"Their sins and their evildoing I will remember no more."

Hebrews 10:17

heart

Imagine Satan saying to Jesus, "Why do you forgive everyone, even the worst sinners, but not me?" Jesus might reply, "Because you never asked from the heart for forgiveness. You never repented."

On hearing this imaginative little exchange, we might look with disdain on the foolish and hard heart of Satan. Yet has each of us asked God from the heart for forgiveness? Do we have a full appreciation of the kind of surrender that such a request involves? Are we ready to submit to the Lordship of Jesus in every part of our lives? Is our repentance total, deep, and sincere, or are we merely repentant for our immediately past sins? Are we primarily motivated by self-interest and removal from divine justice and punishment?

Do we ask forgiveness not only for our transgressions but also for our lack of love for God? Do we repent for our halfhearted and intermittent friendship with Jesus and for our lives, which are too often indistinguishable from those of our non-Christian neighbors?

God wants more than our repentance. He wants our hearts, our love, our very selves. He lavishes his love on the truly humble and contrite heart and, with divine generosity, he remembers our sins no more.

Jesus, your friendship for me is so true, so holy, so complete. It is so open and free; it calls my heart to a joyful surrender. My mind is overwhelmed by the miracle of your personal forgiving love. And yet my commitment dries up by noon—like the morning dew, it disappears. It fades quietly under the press of my frustration and fears. Give me grace, Lord, to sustain my commitment, to cultivate an awareness of your presence, and to place fidelity and loyalty to you above every other person, place, and thing in my life.

SUMMER EVENING

You are my hope, Lord;
my trust, GOD, from my youth...
my hope in you never wavers.

Psalm 71:5-6

Our son Dennis and his wife, Polly, at an early stage in their marriage lived in a small one-bedroom apartment in upper Manhattan. My wife and I had to climb four steep flights of stairs to get to it. It was an Alpine experience. The apartment was a bit cramped, but there was a charming roof-patio off the kitchen.

As we sat on the patio on a summer evening, Dennis talked about his career in the New York theater, the many unfruitful auditions, the long hours of waiting.

He and Polly had set out a number of green and flowering plants around the patio. Dennis shared with us how much he had learned from watching them grow: how they follow patterns of development and how their growth reflects the care that is given. "They taught me to be patient," he said.

When I am anxious and impatient, I think about that summer evening. I believe God was speaking to the four of us gathered there about his plan for lives, about the need to trust in him and to be always open to the feeding and watering of his inspiration and guidance.

Holy Spirit, you are the love of the Father. I know that you were sent by Jesus to teach me all things, to comfort, direct, and guide me. Grant me the grace of patience, cast out my fears and anxieties. Teach me to rest in God's plan for my life at all times, particularly when I am hard-pressed. Give me the peace of Jesus in my heart and in my mind.

plant

ROYAL HOUSEHOLD

...for he is Lord of lords and king of kings,
and those with him are called, chosen,
and faithful.

Revelation 17:14

In our quiet moments, a call to Camelot may ring in our ears, a call to render fealty to the idealized king and queen, to the wise and gentle sovereigns of song and story. Our sense of realism may shatter these sentimentalities, but there may be a deep purpose to our fleeting fascination with royalty.

Jesus is the only true and worthy sovereign. He is royalty realized, deserving of our complete trust and surrender. Jesus, our eternal King, has generously provided us with three thrones before which we can kneel in awe and love.

Our first consideration is the Garden of Gethsemane. Here Jesus experienced fear and dread at his approaching trial, torture, and crucifixion. He desperately wanted to avoid the horrors that awaited him. Yet his love for us was stronger than his fear, and he submitted in love to the cross—to the painful death and public disgrace that saved you and me. The cross of Christ is a throne of love.

Second, we should consider that nothing in human history was more startling and unexpected than the Resurrection of Jesus. It was a unique and miraculous event, the ultimate liberation of the human person. Jesus' rising from the dead assures you and me of forgiveness, salvation, and eternal light. The tomb of Christ is a throne of glory.

Third, consider that Jesus was the power and center of the Christian ministry. He took as apostles ordinary, undistinguished men. He created in them a deep understanding and a strong enduring faith. He gave them power to teach and to heal. Before he ascended into heaven, he inspired them with a vision of a universal religion that would save all generations. The apostles went out from that meeting on the mount to be inspired by the Holy Spirit and to conquer the world for Christ. The Mount of Olives is a throne of victory.

These three thrones call us to awe, adoration, and praise. How far beyond the vision of human love is the stunning reality to which they call us as members of the royal household, as brothers and sisters of the King.

Jesus, no king, no premier, no worldly ruler, has followed your heroic and sublime path of service and sacrifice. You are the Servant/King, the stumbling block of worldly ambition, the vision of every pure heart. May I follow your path of sacrifice, service, and love to glory.

FIRE OF LOVE

"Give me leave to go to my homeland."

Genesis 30:25

Going home—these can be magic words, especially for a soldier on leave, a student at Christmas break, or a missionary flying back for a much needed time of rest. Home can be a warm and soft haven, a harbor for the heart.

Not every home is under God's power and protection, but where Jesus is the head of the house, love fills the home and overflows. When you walk into a home that has been sincerely opened to God's power, you can feel the love—a warmth and vitality of spirit that enfolds you immediately. After a while you feel that, in a sense, you belong to the family group, that you could stay there indefinitely, that you are accepted as someone familiar and beloved.

When you leave a home like that—and a family so full of love—it's like going outdoors on a bitterly cold day. You want to return and warm yourself by the fire of their love. If you can't, some of their love stays with you. It clings and warms. It strengthens you on your way.

Lord Jesus, knowing my unworthiness, I frequently shrink from your love. In my insecurities and fear, I sometimes grasp at your love. I always marvel at your love and its sustaining, strengthening power. Give me the grace, Lord, to give and receive love patiently and freely, even when I don't understand the hearts of others, when I can't perceive their motives and aims clearly. Help me to be able to rest in mystery when necessary and to care with a sincere heart and mind for the people you send to me.

THE POMPEIAN

"But of that day and hour no one knows...."

Matthew 24:36

During the time of the Roman Empire, the city of Pompeii was engulfed in burning lava from an eruption of Mount Vesuvius. At the moment of the tragedy, one Pompeian was kneeling, apparently engaged in some prosaic household task. The body has been preserved in that posture throughout the centuries, incinerated into hardened ash. The figure is strangely compelling, a striking symbol of an interrupted life.

Many people in our society live on the verge of commitment to God. They are reluctant to submit fully. They have not placed themselves decisively under his power and love. They believe that they will surrender to God sometime—but not now.

They live in a state of suspended spirituality. Their vague vision of a reconciliation with God at some indeterminate point in the future may be a deadly illusion. Their journey may be interrupted before they are able to make the one most important decision of their lives.

Dear Jesus, renew your invitation of love and forgiveness to every uncertain heart. Give every man and woman a moment of overwhelming, merciful grace. Draw them close, Lord. Save them.

ruins

SPIRIT AND FLAME

> *"The wind blows where it wills, and you can hear the sound it makes, but you do not know where it comes from or where it goes; so it is with everyone who is born of the Spirit."*
>
> John 3:8

Imagine for a moment looking out a window during a raging storm. You see a small candle burning with a tiny flickering flame in the midst of fierce and gusting winds. Puzzled, you go out into the night and investigate. You perceive that the wind is enveloping the candle, swirling around it, in a strange way protecting the flame.

The human spirit is often and aptly described as a flame, a light that is fragile and luminous but clinging and enduring. The Holy Spirit, the divine life force, is more difficult to picture. Human expression falters, but God generously speaks to our hearts and minds in the second chapter of Acts of the Apostles where the Holy Spirit is described as a mighty wind descending upon the apostles and disciples at Pentecost.

God's greatness and our relative obscurity present a striking dissimilarity. That is the stunning glory of his love for us. It is so unlikely, undeserved, and generous that we find it almost incredible.

To increase your understanding and open your heart more fully to God's love, it may be helpful to think of your spirit as a tiny flame—vulnerable to the buffeting winds of the world but protected, nurtured, and enduring in the center of the mighty winds of God's love.

Father, we experience your creation through our limited senses. The light of our intellect is eager but dim. We barely touch the hem of your garment. We are aware that you always have more for us. Clever evil assaults us daily. Lift us up. Let your light enter deeply into our spirits. Let it become ours so that we can know, think, and act spirit to Spirit, heart to Heart, and love to Love.

CREATING MAGIC

For all of you are children of the light and
children of the day.

1 Thessalonians 5:5

Little Theo proudly showed me his new toy. It consisted of several round colored disks arranged in an overlapping pattern. When the handle of the device was squeezed, the disks whirled around at high speed, creating a vivid pulsating multicolored image. In Theo's little toy, motion created magic.

God calls each of us, always and everywhere, to goodness, caring, compassion, and forgiving; but he respects our freedom. We possess the power to respond to God's calls or to reject them.

Our free acts, our moral choices, weave a spiritual pattern of colors, shadows, and light. Each time we move firmly away from temptation and evil, each time we make a choice for God and goodness, we create a ray of light. Each of these rays is personal and unique. It has its own wavelength.

If we sincerely surrender our hearts to God daily, if we live in an active and personal relationship with him, our acts of love and loyalty will coalesce and create magic. They will merge into a brilliant multicolored image of obedience and fidelity that will please the heart of God.

Father God, you speak to our hearts from your heart. You powerfully draw us to goodness through the power of your Spirit within us. Thank you, Father, for receiving from us the reflected light of your glory.

A SCATTERING OF LOVE

"As I have loved you,
so you also should love one another."

John 13:34

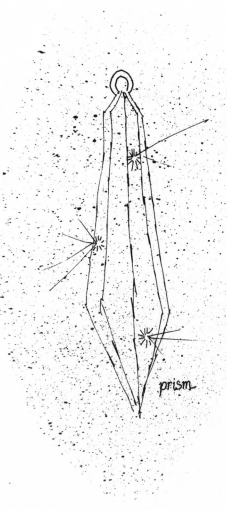

prism

Selinde has placed prisms of transparent crystal in every room in her home. Each one is suspended from a window frame, and when the sun shines, the light entering the crystals separate into the colors of the rainbow. If one of the prisms is nudged, it swings and scatters colors about the room—a dancing revelation of God's artful design in nature.

Receiving unkindness or cruelty from others is painful, hard to endure. Sometimes we can counter these hostile acts with a decently loving Christian response. Sometimes we fail. We try to do it alone. We forget that we possess in our hearts the powerful love of Christ, that through his power in us we can overcome evil with good.

If we yield up our vulnerabilities to Christ—our sensitivities and our sometimes fragile self-image—he will strengthen our efforts to listen, to care, to be present, and to serve and lift up the people we meet. Jesus will help us to be strong, to meet needs through the prism of his example, with a scattering of love.

Father, I am an empty vessel, a dry well, a hollow wall. I echo with pain and self-concern. Without you, I am nothing. You created me out of love. Sustain me with your grace. Fill me with wisdom and power so that I can move outward in strength to those around me, dispensing your love and mercy from a full heart.

THE NEXT STOP

...the Lord knows how to rescue the devout from trial....

2 Peter 2:9

Large problems and major disappointments seldom come into our lives. Small trials and minor frustrations emerge frequently, but we expect them. They are usually controllable, but not always.

Small problems can accumulate forcefully. They can exert pressure like an overwhelming wall of water forcing its slow yet powerful way through a crumbling dike. They can create stressful, draining times that seem unbearable. They can take us to the breaking point.

Speaking of trials and consolation, a wise Franciscan priest told me, "God is love—a love that is always loving—like the sun that is always shining." This beautiful image is a powerful vision of hope. It tells us that God is always there for us but that we may not be open or ready for the reception of his power, that we may not perceive his timing or the purpose and pace of his grace.

If you are now passing through a dark night of the soul, remember that on the other side of the globe the sun is shining. It is there for you. If you are under heavy clouds of discouragement, remember that above the clouds the sun is shining. It is there for you.

If you are now spiritually besieged, if you are under pressure to surrender your personal values and faith, remember that in your heart, vibrantly alive in you, the Son of God is shining spiritually. He is working within you to draw you away from where you are, to move you higher, to draw you closer to him, to empower you to take the next spiritual step in his plan for your life.

waterfall

Jesus, give me the spiritual vision to see beyond my anxieties, fears, and pain. Help me to always seek your plan and purpose in my life, to move forcefully and unafraid into the next step in my walk with you. May I always live in your love and light, sharing with you all the prayers, works, joys, sorrows, trials, and victories of each day.

THE INNER BASE

So we are ambassadors for Christ....

2 Corinthians 5:20

Beautiful, imposing buildings abound on upper Massachusetts Avenue in Washington, D.C. They house the embassies and consulates of many countries. Men and women of worldly power and importance go out daily from these tightly guarded outposts to represent their nations in delicate and difficult negotiations. Because their work is so sensitive, these emissaries must frequently check with their home offices for instructions and guidance.

Every committed Christian is a witness of the Good News of salvation—an ambassador for Christ. God wants to use his emissaries. He has given each of us abundant graces—knowledge, wisdom, and the power to love. These are not fragile gifts to be stored away on a closet shelf. They are gifts for use. They are given to us to be given away. God wants us to cast them forth generously and strongly. The more we give love, support, and understanding to others, the more will God fill us with his gifts and graces.

In the world we sometimes encounter difficult and complex moral challenges. We may need special inspiration and guidance to deal effectively with these situations. We do well to remember that we carry our home office within us and that the voice of the Holy Spirit speaks to our hearts in the fullness of divine wisdom.

The dignity of our vocation may seem too great for us. We may feel unworthy. We are. But God desires—for his purpose—that we be lights in the world as his beloved and empowered ambassadors.

Father God, give me the grace to surrender totally to your call, to cast off every hesitation, to set aside every doubt. I want to be as clay in your holy hands—useful, obedient, and faithful.

CONTRAST

In their distress they cried to the LORD, who...
Led them forth from darkness and gloom
and broke their chains asunder.
Let them thank the LORD for such kindness,
such wondrous deeds for mere mortals.

Psalm 107:13-15

The hot summer sun had set, and my friends and I trudged along the rough path in darkness. It had turned cold and windy, and our sunburned bodies were chilled. I thought how foolish we had been, taking the boat down the river and then horsing around until it capsized and sunk.

Worst of all, our bare feet were sore and bruised. We desperately wanted warmth and rest. Then, far away, I saw a small light. We stepped up our pace and soon were at a farmhouse where we were helped by friendly people.

We are all like the little group I was with that summer night. We sometimes do foolish and thoughtless things that separate us from God and find ourselves in darkness. We trudge along in our daily rounds, feeling stress, becoming psychologically and physically tired.

We need to step up our spiritual pace, to look more keenly, to see that God's light of love and forgiveness is always there for us, that it is there to meet our needs, inform our minds, and strengthen our spirits.

Darkness, stress, the weight of evil in our society, cannot overcome a heart sincerely committed to God. Darkness only makes God's light more vivid—clearer to the eyes of faith.

Jesus, you became sin for me that I might be saved. You, who are Light, entered darkness to set me free. Lord, teach me to avoid even the shadows, teach me to love the light, to remain in your light even when it reveals my sin and weakness. Take away from me, O God, every false pride and pretense. Give me a simple, contrite, and honest heart.

THE QUESTIONS OF CHRIST

*What good is it, my brothers, if someone says
he has faith but does not have works? Can that
faith save him?...So also faith of itself, if it does
not have works, is dead.*

James 2:14, 17

The conference room was empty. I sat alone at the table, looking down the long expanse of shining wood and the twenty empty chairs. How busy this room had been moments ago. How much our meeting had centered on self-interest. How inconclusive and full of posturing it had been. In the final analysis, how little had been accomplished.

Like a character coming on stage, the figure of a window washer appeared outside the window, moving slowly into full view on his automatic scaffold. He washed the windows quickly and efficiently, then ascended silently to the floor above.

His useful and direct labor contrasted strongly with the low productivity of our meeting. I couldn't help but think that the time spent in our meeting could have been redirected to more useful and immediate purposes.

Our spiritual lives may need a change of emphasis—a redirection. We may be too much a student of religion, interested in discussing theology or critiquing liturgy. Or we may be spiritual minimalists, content with a brief morning prayer, Sunday worship, and regular contributions to our local pastor.

These patterns fall short of the call of Christ. There is a deeper level of action and power to which Jesus calls each of us, but we seem to have difficulty hearing his call.

Jesus asks questions:

- "Are you a public Christian in the marketplace in a bold and strong way?"

- "Do you take the initiative to mend broken relationships in your life, particularly in your family?"

- "Have you shared your testimony of faith with your children, particularly your personal spiritual crises and victories."

- "Have you made a personal commitment of your time, resources, and reputation to the cause of Christ and the truths that he taught?"

Jesus calls us to a spiritual life that is deep, mature, and sacrificial, that goes beyond appearances into the heart.

Lord, you know how much I love quiet time with you, how I savor the majesty of the liturgy, and how I rejoice in power-filled preaching and teaching. You also know how I shrink from public witness and service. Make me, Lord, an action person. Teach me to be ready to serve. Help me to see my faith as a personal blessing and a driving force to service and sacrifice.

SUNDAY LESSON

"...there will be one flock, one shepherd."

John 10:16

It was Sunday morning in North Conway, New Hampshire. We had arrived a day earlier and set up our trailer on a large wooded site at the Pine Knoll Campground. We awoke a bit late but managed to get seven children dressed and packed into our station wagon in half an hour.

We arrived at the Catholic church just before ten, and everyone bailed out of the wagon and scampered into church. When we left church after Mass, we discovered that Beth was missing. Since Beth was only nine, we were worried. But in a few minutes she showed up, emerging from the crowd coming out of the Protestant church next door. We all had a good laugh with Beth, who said, "I thought the Mass was a little different."

Looking back at that summer Sunday morning, we can see now the more serious and touching lesson that was in it for all of us. Truly God was teaching us that morning that we are all brothers and sisters under one Father—members of one holy family.

Father God, give me a heart of love and understanding for all Christians. We look to you, Father, to lead us to that unity that will one day bind us all together in spirit, in work, and in one universal Christian witness to the world. Give us also the grace to love and serve all men and women with your heart of compassion and understanding.

MEASURED TIME

Choose life, then, that you and your descendants
may live, by loving the LORD, your God, heeding his
voice, and holding fast to him.

Deuteronomy 30:19-20

Envision a single candle burning with a slow and steady flame. What if you knew your life would last only as long as that candle burned? You would undoubtedly rivet your attention on that flickering light.

Our little analogy may be melodramatic, but it illustrates an important truth that too many of us attempt to ignore. Our life is measured time. It may last longer than a candles' burning, perhaps not.

The young feel immortal. Moments are rich and full, and days—particularly sunny summer days—seem endless. There is time for everything.

Somewhere along the line a change occurs. We experience our mortality through the death of a parent or the serious illness of someone we love. Some people are haunted by these events. Others see them in a Christian light.

Through the teaching of Jesus we know that death is not so much an end as a beginning. It is a transition that will initiate a happier and higher life if we are now living in close friendship with God. The time to deepen and strengthen our relationship with God is now—today—so that when death comes, we will experience not only the sadness of seeing our candle burn out but the overwhelming, unspeakable joy of a face-to-face meeting with our Lord and Savior.

Thank you, Jesus, for your sacrifice on Calvary and your glorious Resurrection. We love you and want to please you in our every thought, word, and deed. Be with us now and when the moment of death comes. Lead us across the chasm into the greater light, into the presence of your Father and the sharing of your glory.

CLOSE HARMONY

*Rather, one is a Jew inwardly, and
circumcision is of the heart, in the spirit, not
the letter....*

Romans 2:29

We constantly send out signals—signs of approval or disapproval. With and without words, we communicate. We draw other men and women in. We rebuff them. We move them around emotionally and intellectually.

Mixed and inconsistent signals from us can confuse others, leaving them uncertain and disturbed. Clear communication depends on the harmonizing of our inner values and purposes with our external actions. We will experience greater freedom and personal power when we turn away from the many ways in which we deceive ourselves and others.

Greater integrity and openness will bring rewards. We may discover an unsuspected lack of love in our hearts or find areas of thriving and subtle sin. Or we may find an inner holiness released, perhaps a renewed or deeper love for others. Whatever the transitions, God will see them. As we begin to move forcefully against our guarded darkness and inner fears, God will send abundant grace to strengthen our repentance, resolve, and growth.

God will heal us and make us whole if we persist and endure in moral courage and openness, in reaching out always to others in sincere love and to ourselves with integrity.

Dear God, we recognize the hazards in our environment. We are vigilant about threats to our physical security. Why do we overlook the enemy within? Why are we fainthearted in love? Lord God, give us light, knowledge, and strength to root out the inner thrust of evil. Help us to integrate and purify our ideas, emotions, and actions, welding them into a holy life.

BARE WOOD

Jesus said to them: "I myself am the bread of life; whoever comes to me will never hunger, and whoever believes in me will never thirst."

John 6:35

When I picked up our old front door at the wood-stripping shop, I was amazed by how completely they had removed the paint. The grain of the bare wood was beautiful, and I anticipated how just the right stain would enhance it.

Our old door was redeemed. It was regenerated and renewed just as we can be if we surrender our lives to Jesus. We may seem irreclaimable to many of the people around us but not to our Lord. He looks beneath the dry, hardened paint of sin. He sees into the bare wood. He perceives our deep and confused hunger for goodness and holiness.

God provides the means for us to turn our lives around. He is pleased when we begin to utilize the grace and light that he sends, when we fearlessly make the right and tough choices. God rejoices when we fill our hunger for goodness— that hunger we were only dimly aware of but that Jesus saw clearly, shining in the bare wood.

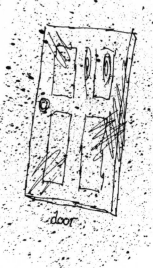

Jesus, fill us with divine fire. Activate our moral courage, sharpen our vision and strengthen our wills. Give us the grace, the moral eye, to see our dignity and glory through your eyes—to know what we can become through your grace in us.

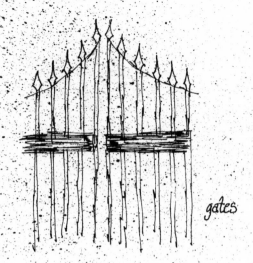

gates

THRONE OF GLORY

And now, children, remain in him, so that
when he appears we may have confidence and
not be put to shame by him at his coming.

1 John 2:28

"Virtue is so rare that it should be used sparingly."
Unfortunately, the cynical humor in this statement reflects much that is true about human behavior. Some
people do measure out their love and mercy in a miserly
way. The gates of their souls are open just a trifle.

They are spiritually guarded and fearful, knowing
that generosity of spirit involves vulnerability. They
seek holiness without risk, sanctity without sacrifice,
and salvation without surrender. They want to open
their hearts to God and to others in a prudent, careful,
and measured way.

They are bargaining with God. Their lives ask the
question "How little can I do and still be saved?" They
have set up an arm's-length relationship with Jesus
Christ. Every hour of every day, they pass up the
opportunity for complete surrender to Christ, for estab-
lishing intimacy as the basis for their relationship with
God.

They will come naked and empty-handed to the
Judgment. The only baggage we can bring to God is faith,
trust, works of mercy, and acts of love in his name. What
we will face finally is not a bargaining table but a throne of
glory.

Jesus, your great gift of freedom and choice has meaning. It
is not a sham or a game. We know that you are love and
light but also justice. Our free choices, our smallest acts,
have eternal value. They can be pleasing in your sight or
vile. That is our risk. But I thank you, dear Jesus, that it
can also be our salvation, our glory, and our victory.

OPEN HEARTS

"Take care, then, how you hear. To anyone who has, more will be given, and from the one who has not, even what he seems to have will be taken away."

Luke 8:18

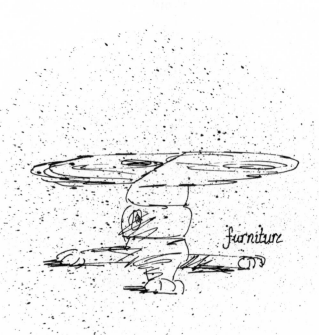

furniture

Wood veneering, the bonding of precious wood panels to the exterior surfaces of frames made of ordinary wood, is a useful technique. It makes attractive, precious wood furniture more widely available at a reasonable price. Yet it remains a substitute, something less than the real thing.

We may desire to have solid oak furniture in our dining rooms, but it is not essential. In our hearts, though, in our seeking God's truth, we want the real thing.

God's truth has been fragmented and distorted in a multitude of ways over the centuries. Seeing this, many have become cynical. They ask, "Whom shall we believe?" Some men and women despair. They ask, "Is there no credible witness?" Some people retreat to narrow individualism. They state with strong emphasis, "I know the truth. I'll interpret it my way."

God sees the predicament we have created for ourselves, and he responds in love. He teaches his truth through his Church and—vividly and dramatically—through the lives of "living saints."

He speaks the truth to our inner hearts through inspiration. Most fully and eloquently, he teaches us through the Bible. We learn about Jesus, the Son of God, the depth of power of his love and sacrifice, his public disgrace and his final victory, which he calls us to share.

Through all these channels, God calls the sincere and surrendered heart forward. We can be certain of one thing: God neither deceives us nor permits a pure heart to be deceived. A heart open in worship and a mind seeking the truth will hear his words truly and his call clearly.

Jesus, the people I meet every day know so little about me that is really important. You, Lord, know my inner heart. You know my continuing hunger for more and more of your truth and love. Send me, Lord, not only your truth but the power to act with Christian wisdom, conviction, and courage. Strengthen me to act on your truth and to persevere—and not to count the cost.

SAVING AND BEING SAVED

*And his commandment is this: we should
believe in the name of his Son, Jesus Christ,
and love one another just as he commanded us.*

1 John 3:23

Jeff stalked away in anger. Something I had said
innocently had somehow upset him. He came to me
later and we talked about it. He said, "I want to ask your
forgiveness for my misinterpretation of what you said
and for walking off in anger. I want to set myself right
with the Lord."

I was pleased with our reconciliation but felt there
was something wrong, something incomplete about it.
It finally came to me. Jeff's repentance was primarily
egocentric. The bottom-line focus was on him and his
salvation. He had said very little about my feelings or
our relationship. When I asked Jeff about it, he con-
fessed that his motivation had been primarily self-
centered.

It is shocking to realize how often we relate—even
to God—in a self-centered way. In dealing with our
sins, we tend to focus on being removed from jeopardy,
on saving ourselves. In cases where we have been
severely wronged by another, how difficult it is to pray
for that person or to seek reconciliation.

We fail to see sin for what it is—a failure of love and
a rupture of a relationship. Repentance can only be
complete when we have made our best effort to reestab-
lish the relationship.

Despite its great importance, being saved should
never be our central goal. It should be a by-product of
love and reconciliation, of our saving and being saved.

Father God, my fear of losing your favor is sometimes greater than my love for you and for my brothers and sisters in Christ. Give me the grace to see that my salvation and fulfillment is in and through you and through the men and women you send into my life. Give me a continuing awareness of your cherishing love and your call to unity. You showed us on Calvary the supreme reconciling power of sacrifice. Teach us to love one another.

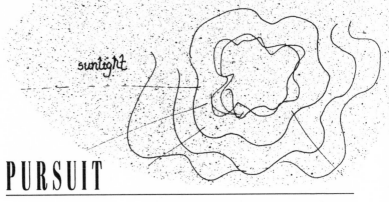

PURSUIT

The LORD, the God of gods,
has spoken and summoned the earth
from the rising of the sun to its setting.

Psalm 50:1

Sunlight on a summer's day has power. Sometimes the sun is so strong and bright on the beach or on the water that we have to close our eyes. Yet strangely enough, even through closed eyes we can still see light. Try it; it's true. Strong, direct sunlight is the only thing we can see with our eyes closed.

God's grace is like that strong light from the sun. We can close our eyes, our minds, and our hearts to God's healing power, but we can't keep it out. God never gives up. He never withdraws his light and his love. He tracks us always—lovingly but relentlessly.

The worst sinner, in the deepest moments of perversity, can testify that God persists, that as he convicts the sinner he mercifully sends out an invitation to change, a caring call to forgiveness and inner peace.

The light of heaven pierces every darkness. It reaches every heart. You and I are wanted men and women. We are pursued by love forever.

Lord God, we read in Scripture that you are love. We see
your grace and light in our lives. Yet we temporize, we
evade your invitation, your forgiveness, your compassion
and love. Thank you, Lord, for your patience and power,
for your victory in every heart that wisely surrenders to
your loving call.

MORNING MOTH

Good and upright is the LORD,
who shows sinners the way.

Psalm 25:8

I awoke in the semidarkness of the camping trailer. In the early dawn, Glacier National Park was quiet and peaceful. Looking up, I could see light through the vented aperture in the ceiling. It was screened, and a small moth was vainly trying to reach the brighter light outside. The moth tried again and again until, finally, it perched immobile on the screen.

How many people are battering their spiritual wings against a screen of temptation and peer pressure that frequently seems overwhelming? How many give up and become morally immobile, paralyzed with fear, discouragement, and indecision?

God sees our problems and predicaments. He wants to release us from our moral dilemmas, but he needs our help and cooperation. Unlike the moth, we have the power to select and the freedom to make judgments. We know where help can be found.

We can feed on God's word in Scripture. We can attend to the teaching voice of the Church. We can study the lives of strong Christian people. We can pray, humbly and with a trusting heart.

Through these turnings to God, we will enhance our spiritual sensitivity and bring to light the subtle sin in our lives. We will develop moral power and closeness to God. We will cooperate with him in our healing and regeneration. Our freedom has a purpose and a glory.

Father, by the light of your Holy Spirit, you send us truth, guidance, and direction. We receive words of wisdom from your Church. You send inspiration and example in the men and women you place near us. Your blessings and gifts are without number. We thank you most of all, Father, for freedom, for the power to turn to you and to work in harmony with your love.

WRAPPINGS

"By this is my Father glorified, that you bear much fruit and become my disciples."

John 15:8

As the woman opened the beautifully wrapped box and took out the gift, expectant and happy faces awaited her reaction. I could see her hesitation and confusion. She was somewhat disappointed but didn't want to show it. Finally, she feigned delight in the gift and everyone was satisfied.

The human criteria for selecting gifts are unclear and uncertain. We try to guess what will please another person or perhaps pick out something that we would like to have. We can never be sure that we have just the right gift, one that will be pleasing.

The gifts of God are different. They are designed by his divine mind to delight our hearts unerringly, but they call for a clear response from us.

God's gifts are inherently active, dynamic, and fruitful. They are intended for use. They are meant to be an extension of God's work in the world—through us. God may send the gift of love for the poor, for example; but the recipient, while feeling beneficent toward the poor, may fail to translate his or her love into service and sacrifice, which is love's real name. The gift of love is then trapped in the wrapped box—unopened, unused, and sterile.

Be ready and eager to serve your God, to tear off and discard the wrappings on his gifts so that his power and purpose may be made visible and fruitful in you and in your life.

Holy Spirit, I find it easy to reflect on the high and the holy, the noble and the pure, on God's mercy and goodness to me. Help me to have an equal love for action. Inspire me to step out into the cold winds of the marketplace, to be faithful and constant in good works, service, and sacrifice.

GREG

"...and I will be a father to you,
and you shall be sons and daughters to me,
says the Lord Almighty."

2 Corinthians 6:18

When Greg graduated from high school, he was fortunate. He got a well-paying job right away. He was young and had money in his pocket. Life was easy and sweet.

In light of Greg's new status, his dad levied a room-and-board payment on him. Greg was angry. He thought, *This is my home. Why should I be paying rent?* But he didn't object openly.

A few years later, Greg's job situation improved substantially. He began to look ahead and thought seriously about buying a house. "It will take me a little time to get enough together for the down payment," he told his dad, "but I am pretty clear on the kind of place I want."

"Greg," his dad replied, "the money you've been giving us for room and board—well, I've been putting it away for you. It should take care of your down payment." Greg was stunned. Tears welled up in his eyes. He said incredulously, "You were helping me all the time, and I was so mad about it. I'm sorry, Dad. I didn't understand."

Too many of us don't understand that God our Father helps us all the time. We take our life, our breath, our faith, and the love that surrounds us for granted. We forget that it is God's grace that covers us, that sustains us in difficulties and guards us in dangers.

How blessed are the moments of clarity and realism when we remember that God our Father is our life, our love, and our power, that we survive and prosper because he has been helping us all the time.

Father in heaven, you are my God. You give me the grace to live in a truly Christian way. Let me never forget who I am and whose I am. Let me taste daily the joy and peace of knowing and serving you with thanksgiving. Let that be my reward.

THE LISTENING GOD

The mouths of the just utter wisdom;
their tongues speak what is right.

Psalm 37:30

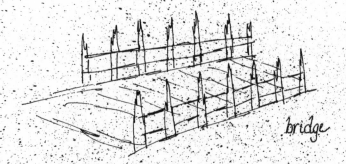

bridge

The little bridge, made of rough timbers, stood in a deep valley several miles from our campsite.

My grandson Isaac and I stood on the bridge in the dusk and looked down the long shadowed space. I couldn't help but wonder, *Where does the valley lead? What is at its end—a rainbow or a dismal swamp?*

We felt very much alone in the quiet gathering dimness. Suddenly, Isaac let out a shout: "Hello-o-o!" After an almost imperceptible moment, his voice returned to us in echoing waves, "Hello-lo-lo-lo!"

Isaac laughed with delight. Then I tried it, and we enjoyed playing echo chamber for a while before returning to our campsite.

All of us live on a spiritual bridge, and our thoughts, words, and deeds shout down a valley creating echoes. Our messages echo powerfully. Love begets love. When we reach out sensitively and tenderly to others, they invariably return our concern and affection. When we despise and reject others, they usually retaliate with hatred and malice. When we are indifferent to others, they draw away from us. Then we experience loneliness.

We have the power to create and form the psychological and spiritual climate that surrounds us. How foolish the man or woman who shouts hatred and rejection down the valley then weeps because his or her life is lacking love.

God shares in every part of our lives. He shouts down the valley, too. But the echo he waits to hear is not his own voice but our voice answering him in love, surrender, and joy.

Dear God, give us grace to love and to accept love, to be patient and strong, to be wise and forgiving. Help us to sweeten and strengthen all of our relationships by being Christ to one another. Help us also to see Christ in one another even in the most difficult and trying times.

PATH OF GLORY

*...after laying the cross on him [Simon], they
made him carry it behind Jesus.*

Luke 23:26

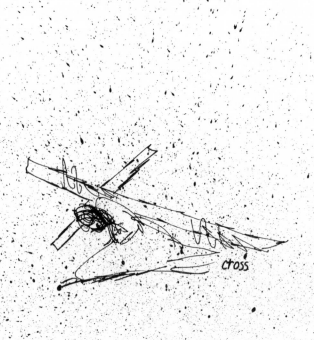

cross

As Christians, we may prosper in the world, or we may be poor. We may be respected and loved for our Christianity, or we may be despised and rejected because of it. When we pray for healing, our physical illnesses and problems may or may not be removed. God does not assure us of worldly success or freedom from pain.

The basic challenge of the Christian life is a personal call for love and loyalty to Jesus. The rewards he offers are inner peace and eternal salvation—complete unity with him.

Jesus knows our problems. He has experienced our pain and discouragement. He has warned us what to expect from the world and from our own weakness. He lovingly and generously sends help—adequate graces to sustain us in spiritual courage, moral endurance, and personal loyalty to him.

He says to each of us, "My beloved, your cross, so oppressive, painful, and exhausting—embrace it. It will be your way out as it was mine."

How many Christians fall prey to prosperity theology, to imperious demands for physical healing, to using God to meet our perception of our needs? Through these errors many of us evade our path of glory. We flee the crosses in our lives, not realizing that embracing and overcoming them is, for us, the true imitation of Christ.

"In your heart, you can carry your crosses with Jesus. You can walk beside him on the way. And perhaps, even in the depth of his pain, you will see him turn to you with a loving, fleeting glance that will remain with you forever."

Dear Jesus, what is life without love? love without commitment? commitment with sacrifice? sacrifice without fulfillment? Dear Savior, you are my fulfillment, my joy, and my strength. Receive my fidelity. Hold me close.

ABOUT THE AUTHOR

Leo Holland was formerly director of Management Policy for the Department of Health and Human Services and administrator of the National Service Committee for the Catholic Charismatic Renewal. He is a retired Lieutenant Colonel in the United States Army. The father of seven children and grandfather of twelve, Mr. Holland currently lives in St. Petersburg, Florida, with his wife, Wyona.

If you found *Piercing the Mist: Glimpses of God in the Wonders of Life* to be inspiring and spiritually enriching, you may also enjoy reading *Illuminations: Meditations for Seeing God in our World* by Leo Holland, also published by Liguori Publications.